Focus on Bridge Defence

Further outstanding defence plays from the championships

Focus on Bridge Defence

Further
outstanding defence
plays from the championships

Aksel J. Nielsen

EDITED BY

Douglas Munro

Kaye & Ward
LONDON

First published in Great Britain by
Kaye & Ward Ltd,
21 New Street, London EC2M 4NT
1980

ISBN 0 7182 1233 9

Phototypeset in V.I.P. Baskerville
by Western Printing Services Ltd, Bristol.
Printed and bound in Great Britain
by Redwood Burn Limited
Trowbridge & Esher

Prologue

When Ely Culbertson published in 1934, his *Red Book of Play* he very sensibly included a chapter on defence. In this he gave several summaries of leads from various combinations of cards, played in different situations and circumstances, as well as drawing attention to other more general rules, and giving advice about the strategy defenders could use. Most of what he wrote still holds good after 45 years; his rules and advice were absorbed by beginners at the game and, as a result, are now known by all present day bridge players.

However, nobody could achieve any distinction by simply following these fundamentals, and perhaps we have here the reason why all later writers of bridge books and magazine articles were rather inclined to put emphasis on declarer's play and to ignore defence. This seemed to me to be very wrong and I have felt for a long time that the study of defence hands should be accepted as a much more valid subject of interest.

For quite obvious reasons good defence demands skilled play from the declarer, because the standard of play can never be a one-sided matter; indeed the reverse is very much the case. So when, in 1948, I published my first book (incidentally written in Danish) I gave it a title which translates as *Defence: the step-child of Bridge*. Perhaps I should mention here that this was *the first book in any language* on this aspect of the game, it was reprinted in 1976, with a variation in the title.

Since 1948 times have changed and by 1955 when my second book was published (and this was a collection of a 100 new defence hands) defence was no longer 'the step-child of Bridge'. Quite the contrary now, for it had come to be realised by all writers on bridge that defence hands are *the most instructive*, for the very good reason that not only defender's but also declarer's play is vitally involved, frequently showing how declarer should *not* have played!

This present book, my fourth collection of defence hands, has 138 of them, played by 194 experts, from 20 countries and I

5

should stress that none of these hands are to be found in either of my first two Danish books or in *Defence at Bridge* which was written in collaboration with Victor Mollo, and published in 1976.

Some of the hands I have included here will no doubt be more interesting than others; but all, I think, are instructive. I would suggest that the reader should first look at the two hands only, and try to solve the problem posed, before turning overleaf to see how the defending hand was played in the actual game and by whom, as well as when and where. In many cases he may quickly find the correct solution, but in others some imagination may be needed to guess what the defender did to find his really killing mode of play, or a lead that would fool the declarer into going down in a cold contract.

I have not divided the hands into similar groups which would illustrate one style of defence, but instead have so arranged them that no single hand can give any indication of what will be the outcome of the next hand. I should add here that in this collection there is just one hand that does *not* show a defence that killed the contract; it illustrates an imaginative defence that *could* perhaps have led to such a killing. Had it been made, and had it succeeded (the possibility of which we will never know now) it would have completely changed the result of the World Championship in Bermuda in 1975! I wonder if you can recognise it?

AKSEL J. NIELSEN

Defence plays are included from the following:

THE NUMBERS ARE THOSE OF THE SOLUTIONS

7

Soerensen, Asger *81*   Weje, Christian Nymann *97*
Voigt, Axel *12*   Werdelin, Stig *11, 30, 129*
Wille-Joergensen, Gudrun *118*

Egypt
Sharif, Omar *4*

Eire
Johnson, A. H. *3*

Finland
Kaitera, Mrs. I. *76*   Lindén, Mrs Siv *76*

France
Caralli, Théodore *13*   Jaïs, Pierre *13, 83*
Cohen, Gilles *69*   Lévy, G. *80*
Delorme, Jacques *63*   Paoli, Mado *86, 126*
Deschapelles, Guillaume le   Pariente, Fanny *126*
Breton *66*   Pilon, Dominique *47*
Desrousseaux, Gérard *34, 74*   Poubeau, Dominique *99*
Devriès, Madeleine *34*   Roudinesco, Marc *36, 50*
Duca, Cino del *91*   Schneider, Marc *119*
Guitton, Charles *83*   Stoppa, Jean-Louis *36*
Temime, Jean-Pierre *130*

Germany
Chodziesner, Fritz *81*   Dewitz, Egmont von *59*
Pressburger, John *128*

Great Britain
Amsbury, Joe *85*   McLaren, John *136*
Forrester, Tony *44*   Reese, Terence *20*
Gardener, Nico *42*   Rimington, Derek *29*
Gardener, Nicola *65*   Rodrigue, Claude *79, 108*
Hoffman, Martin *59*   Schapiro, Boris *20, 109*
Jackson, Howard *32*   Shenkin, Barnet *21, 26*
Konstam, Kenneth *108*   Smolski, Roman *44*
Markus, Rixi *41*   Sowter, Tony *85*
Mayer, Edward *105*   Tarlo, Louis *42, 79*

8

Holland

Kreijns, Hans *12, 62* Rijke, A. *33*
Oudshoorn, Leo *33* Slavenburg, Cornelius *12, 62*

Hungary

Darvas, Robert *87*

Israel

Elenberg, Izhak *13*

Italy

Belladonnia, Giorgio *1,3,5,60,* Giovine, Michele *28*
138 Pabis-Ticci, Camillo *39*
Forquet, Pietro *2, 13, 19* Ritis, Bruno de *106*
Franco, Arturo *89* Rota, Ottavio *38*
Galla, Vittorio La *106* Vivaldi, Antonio *132*
Garozzo, Benito *1, 2, 4, 5, 19,*
39, 60, 105, 138

New Zealand

Kerr, Roy *49*

Norway

Boe, Rolf *61* Marstrander, Peter *122*
Christiansen, Leif *52* Mikkelsen, Sverre *57*
Falck-Pedersen, Leif *52* Nielsen, Isak *18*
Jormann, Oscar *18* Pihl, Mrs *97*
Larsen, Robert *84* Stabell, Leif Erik *122*

Poland

Lebodia, Lukasz *31* Wilkosz, Andrzej *31*

Sweden

Eriksson, Karin *24* Kruisenstierna, Douglas von *54*
Friberg, Elna *54* Maartensson, Eva *24*
Gullberg, Tommy *23* Mattsson, Goeran *100*
Hoeglund, Lars *23* Sjoeberg, Aake *6*
Jannersten, Eric *92* Wennberg, Seth *53*

9

Switzerland

Arndt, Mrs *98*   Besse, Jean *124*
Bernasconi, Pietro *125*   Kutner, Yvonne *98*
Trad, Tony *124*

USA

Allinger, Paul *113*
Andersen, Ron *134*
Baron, Arthur *72*
Becker, B. Jay *73*
Bishop, Clifford W. *50*
Blinder, Alvin *13*
Bowie, Clagett *125*
Crane, Barry *120*
Crawford, John R. *95*
Donelly, Jack *37*
Ehrlenbach, Jack *16*
Eisenberg, William *8, 27, 90*
Ellenby, Milton *66*
Farrell, Mary Jane *22, 58*
Fishbein, Harry *78*
Frey, Richard L. *134*
Goldman, Robert *8, 90, 127*
Goren, Charles H. *45*
Hamman, Robert *7, 60*
Heitner, Paul *116*
Ignatz, Bennie *105*
Jacoby, James *8*
Jacoby, Oswald *81, 123*
Jordan, Robert *46, 64*
Lavinthal, Hy *90*
Lavinthal, Sylvia *112*
Lawrence, Michael *7, 101, 127*
Lazard, Sidney *96*
Leventritt, Peter *56*
Lipsitz, Bobby *117*
Long, May-Belle *13*
Lowenthal, John *116*
McKenney, Wm. E. *134*

McWilliams, Bill *25, 78*
Michaels, Terry *107*
Mott-Smith, Geoffrey *35*
Oakie, Donald *70*
Pavlicek, Richard *115*
Rapee, George *123*
Rebner, Stella *107*
Robinson, Arthur *64*
Robinson, Stephen *13*
Root, William *55, 104*
Roth, Alvin *55, 104*
Rubens, Jeff *73*
Rubin, Ira *18*
Schenken, Howard *56*
Scheuer, Jerome *102*
Schleifer, Meyer *50, 70*
Sobel, Alexander M. *107*
Sobel, Helen *107*
Solomon, Peggy *22*
Soloway, Paul *27*
Sontag, Alan *77, 121*
Spotts, Robert L. *101*
Stayman, Sam *103*
Steen, Douglas *71*
Sullivan, Dennis *50*
Travers, Mrs C. E. *45*
Turner, Gloria *66*
Walsh, Richard *88*
Wei, Kathie *134*
Weichsel, Peter *121*
Weiss, Larry *14*
Wolff, Robert *8, 60*
Woods, Mrs A. H. *13*

10

Championship Defence Hands

Deal Number 1

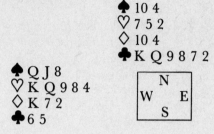

                    ♠ 10 4
                    ♡ 7 5 2
                    ◇ 10 4
                    ♣ K Q 9 8 7 2
♠ Q J 8
♡ K Q 9 8 4   N
◇ K 7 2   W   E
♣ 6 5   S

Dealer South. East–West vulnerable
The bidding:
        South   North
        1 NT   3 NT

West leads the ♡Q, in accordance with the Roman system as
well as with Rusinow, being the lowest of two touching honours. With the ♡10 East denies the jack. West switches to the
♠Q and ♠J, both holding, East following with the ♠3 and ♠2.
What now?

Deal Number 2

                    ♠ 5 4
                    ♡ A J 6 5 2
                    ◇ K 7 5 3
                    ♣ 8 5
                                    ♠ 9 8 7 3 2
                    N   ♡ Q 8 3
                W   E   ◇ 8
                    S   ♣ K Q 9 6

South/North–South.
The bidding:
South   North
1 NT   3 ♡
3 NT

West leads the ♠Q. Declarer wins with the ace and plays the ♡10. West covers with the king. Dummy wins with the ace and continues with the ♡2. How does East plan the defence?

Deal Number 3

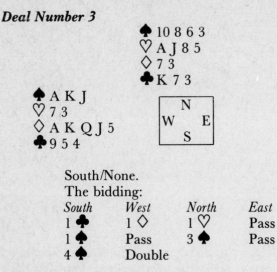

```
              ♠ 10 8 6 3
              ♡ A J 8 5
              ◇ 7 3
              ♣ K 7 3
♠ A K J                    N
♡ 7 3                 W        E
◇ A K Q J 5                S
♣ 9 5 4
```

South/None.
The bidding:

South	West	North	East
1 ♣	1 ◇	1 ♡	Pass
1 ♠	Pass	3 ♠	Pass
4 ♠	Double		

West leads the ◇K and continues with the ace. Declarer ruffs with the ♠4 and plays a club to dummy's king to lead the ♠3 and finesse with the ♠9. How does West plan the defence?

Solution Number 1

```
                    ♠ 10 4
                    ♡ 7 5 2
                    ◇ 10 4
Belladonna          ♣ K Q 9 8 7 2    Garozzo
♠ Q J 8                      N        ♠ K 5 3 2
♡ K Q 9 8 4             W        E    ♡ 10 3
◇ K 7 2                      S        ◇ A J 9 5
♣ 6 5                                 ♣ J 10 4
                    ♠ A 9 7 6
                    ♡ A J 6
                    ◇ Q 8 6 3
                    ♣ A 3
```

Match in Taipei just after the World Championships, 1971,

between the USAces who had just won the championships and
a team partly consisting of players from the Italian 'blue' team
who had not played in the championships.

North went to 3 No Trumps in the hope of six club tricks.

Belladonna led the ♡Q, the lowest of two touching honours,
and with the ♡10 Garozzo denied the ♡J. Belladonna switched
to the ♣Q and ♣J, both winning, whilst Garozzo made a mild
come-on with the ♣3 and ♣2.

At this point in the game Belladonna sat thoughtfully for
some time. He finally came to the conclusion that declarer
could not be completely 'dead' in spades as he had ducked the
first heart. It was very probable that he was now holding a
tenace in spades and so expected to get his ninth trick if
Belladonna continued in that suit. In consequence Belladonna
switched again, but this time to the ◊2. Garozzo went up with
the ◊A and continued with the ◊J, and so secured three
diamond tricks for the defence and setting the contract.

Solution Number 2

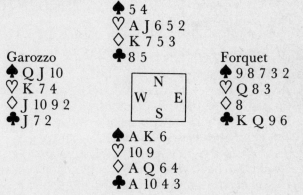

Garozzo / Forquet hand diagram:

Dummy (North):
♠ 5 4
♡ A J 6 5 2
◊ K 7 5 3
♣ 8 5

West (Garozzo):
♠ Q J 10
♡ K 7 4
◊ J 10 9 2
♣ J 7 2

East (Forquet):
♠ 9 8 7 3 2
♡ Q 8 3
◊ 8
♣ K Q 9 6

South:
♠ A K 6
♡ 10 9
◊ A Q 6 4
♣ A 10 4 3

A Teams-of-four Match France-Italy, Cannes, 1968.

Contract: 3 No Trumps. Lead ♣Q.

Declarer won with the ♣A and played the ♡10. The question should, perhaps, have already been asked about West's
defence, but the reader will be aware that Benito Garozzo
covered with the ♡K. Declarer won with dummy's ace and
continued with the ♡2. It was now up to Pietro Forquet. He
ducked with the ♡8, and so dummy's hearts were blocked.

Notwithstanding declarer tried to establish two entries in diamonds so as to utilise the hearts, but as this was quite impossible he had to go down one.

It will be well understood that this stopping of the double finesse is quite elementary, but nevertheless it was missed by West at the other table as the result of which declarer made four quite easily.

Solution Number 3

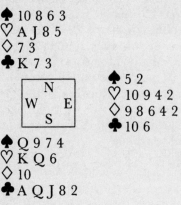

```
                        ♠ 10 8 6 3
                        ♡ A J 8 5
                        ◇ 7 3
                        ♣ K 7 3
       Belladonna
       ♠ A K J                        ♠ 5 2
       ♡ 7 3            N             ♡ 10 9 4 2
       ◇ A K Q J 5    W   E           ◇ 9 8 6 4 2
       ♣ 9 5 4          S             ♣ 10 6
                        ♠ Q 9 7 4
                        ♡ K Q 6
                        ◇ 10
                        ♣ A Q J 8 2
```

Practising in Italy, 1969.

Contract: 4♠ doubled. Lead ◇K, then ◇A.

Declarer ruffed the second diamond and went to dummy on the ♣K to play the ♣3 and finesse with the ♣9.

Belladonna went right up with the ace and continued with the ◇Q for a ruff and discard!!

Declarer was not completely fooled. He reasoned that Belladonna would also be holding the ♠K, but not, of course, the ♠J. So he ruffed in dummy and played the ♠10 for a new finesse. Then Giorgio Belladonna won with the ♠J and drew the remaining trumps with the ♠K. He then cashed the two long diamonds, and the contract was down three.

Deal Number 4

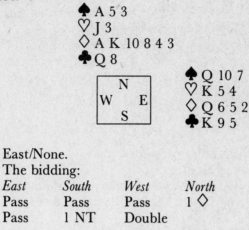

♠ A 5 3
♡ J 3
◇ A K 10 8 4 3
♣ Q 8

♠ Q 10 7
♡ K 5 4
◇ Q 6 5 2
♣ K 9 5

East/None.
The bidding:

East	South	West	North
Pass	Pass	Pass	1 ◇
Pass	1 NT	Double	

West leads the ♡10 and East wins the trick with the king. How does East continue?

Deal Number 5

♠ J
♡ Q 7 6 3
◇ 9 8 6 5
♣ J 6 4 2

♠ A Q 8 7
♡ A K 10 9 4
◇ A 7
♣ 9 3

East/Both.
The bidding:

East	South	West	North
1 ♣	Pass	1 ◇	Pass
1 ♡	1 ♠	Pass	Pass
Double			

West leads the ♡5. How does East plan the defence?

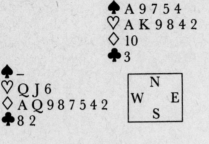

♠ A 9 7 5 4
♡ A K 9 8 4 2
♢ 10
♣ 3

♠ –
♡ Q J 6
♢ A Q 9 8 7 5 4 2
♣ 8 2

West/North–South.
The bidding:

West	North	East	South
5 ♢	5 ♡	Pass	6 ♣

West's opening lead is the ♢A to which East follows with the ♢6 and South with the ♢J. What now?

Solution Number 4

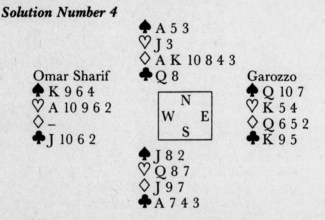

♠ A 5 3
♡ J 3
♢ A K 10 8 4 3
♣ Q 8

Omar Sharif
♠ K 9 6 4
♡ A 10 9 6 2
♢ –
♣ J 10 6 2

Garozzo
♠ Q 10 7
♡ K 5 4
♢ Q 6 5 2
♣ K 9 5

♠ J 8 2
♡ Q 8 7
♢ J 9 7
♣ A 7 4 3

Summer Festival at Deauville, about 1970.
Contract: 1 No Trump doubled. Lead ♡10.
Benito Garozzo won the trick with the ♡K and seeing all dummy's tricks he wondered whether he had been too confident in converting Omar Sharif's absolute take-out-double. He decided, however, to attack dummy's entry and led the ♣Q.
Declarer won with dummy's ace and then made the mistake of putting down the ♢A instead of a low diamond, for it then

became impossible to set up that suit for the very good reason that Garozzo ducked when a low diamond was next led to the jack in the closed hand. Thus Garozzo was able to stop the suit. In desperation declarer then led a low club to dummy's queen, but Garozzo won with the king and switched to spades. So the contract went down two.

Solution Number 5

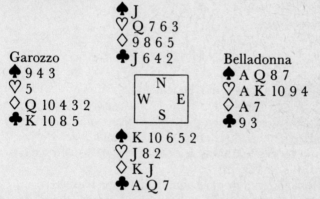

Garozzo
♠ 9 4 3
♡ 5
◇ Q 10 4 3 2
♣ K 10 8 5

Belladonna
♠ A Q 8 7
♡ A K 10 9 4
◇ A 7
♣ 9 3

North:
♠ J
♡ Q 7 6 3
◇ 9 8 6 5
♣ J 6 4 2

South:
♠ K 10 6 5 2
♡ J 8 2
◇ K J
♣ A Q 7

Match in Dublin against a strong visiting precision team, January 1973.

Contract 1♠ doubled. Lead ♡5.

Giorgio Belladonna won with the ♡K and switched to the ♣9 to make it easier for Benito Garozzo to exit later! Declarer ducked and Garozzo won with the ♣K and continued with the ♣10. Declarer won in the closed hand and played the ♠2 to dummy's jack.

Belladonna won with the ♣Q. Now it was the time to cash the ♡A and then to lead a low heart, Garozzo ruffed and played a club; Belladonna promptly ruffed to continue with a fourth round of hearts. Declarer then ruffed with the ♠10, and Garozzo unblocked the ♠9 by underruffing. If he had not done so he would have been endplayed in the next trick. Now Belladonna held the trump tenace and could exit in hearts. As a result declarer had to play the diamonds from the closed hand, and consequently won only two trump tricks and one club trick. Down four!

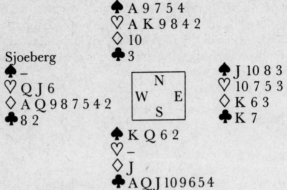

Don Pepe International Tournament, Marbella, Spain, 1971.
Contract: 6♣.

In contrast to other players who are mentioned who had underled their top honours, and which would have been equally successful in this deal, Sjoeberg of Sweden put down his ◇A. But what then?

From his own goulash hand Sjoeberg had the feeling that declarer might be void in hearts and might, therefore, try to enter dummy in spades so as to be able to finesse an eventual trump honour through East. And so he continued with the ◇2 for a ruff and discard. But declarer could not make use of the ruff in dummy, because if he did he would lose the trump lead and finesse. He therefore ruffed in the closed hand and led the ♠2.

This, clearly, was what Sjoeberg was hoping for. He ruffed and again led a diamond. Declarer was resigned to the fact that he could not enter dummy in spades, and so he again ruffed in the closed hand in order to draw the ♣A. The king, however, did not drop and the contract went down two.

Deal Number 7

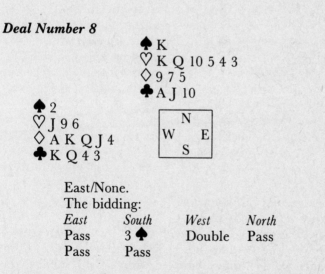

♠ Q J 5 2
♡ 5
♢ Q 3
♣ K Q 6 4 3 2

♠ 10 3
♡ K 7 6 3 2
♢ A 10 9 8
♣ 8 7

North/East–West.
The bidding:

North	South
Pàss	4 ♡

West leads the ♢A and continues with the ♢10, East having followed with the ♢7. East wins with the ♢K and switches to the ♣J. Declarer wins with the ♣A and leads the ♡A and then the ♡8 and ♡9. How does West continue the defence?

Deal Number 8

♠ K
♡ K Q 10 5 4 3
♢ 9 7 5
♣ A J 10

♠ 2
♡ J 9 6
♢ A K Q J 4
♣ K Q 4 3

East/None.
The bidding:

East	South	West	North
Pass	3 ♠	Double	Pass
Pass	Pass		

West draws the ♢K, East following with the ♢2 and declarer with the ♢6. What is West's next lead?

Deal Number 9

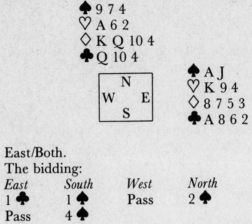

♠ 9 7 4
♡ A 6 2
◇ K Q 10 4
♣ Q 10 4

♠ A J
♡ K 9 4
◇ 8 7 5 3
♣ A 8 6 2

East/Both.
The bidding:

East	South	West	North
1 ♣	1 ♠	Pass	2 ♠
Pass	4 ♠		

West leads the ♣9 and the ♣4 is played from dummy. How does East plan the defence?

Solution Number 7

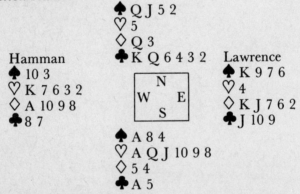

♠ Q J 5 2
♡ 5
◇ Q 3
♣ K Q 6 4 3 2

Hamman
♠ 10 3
♡ K 7 6 3 2
◇ A 10 9 8
♣ 8 7

Lawrence
♠ K 9 7 6
♡ 4
◇ K J 7 6 2
♣ J 10 9

♠ A 8 4
♡ A Q J 10 9 8
◇ 5 4
♣ A 5

Life Master Pairs at Boston, 1970.
  Contract: 4♡. Lead ◇A.
  Michael Lawrence followed with the ◇7, won the next trick with the ◇K, and switched to the ♣J. Declarer won with the ♣A, cashed the ♡A and continued with the ♡8, holding the trick. He then played the ♡9.
  This time Robert Hamman won with the ♡K and led the

♣8, with the inevitable result that dummy was blocked. Declarer therefore tried the ♣Q from dummy, but Lawrence ducked and thus prevented a re-entry in spades. In sheer desperation declarer now had to hope that the last club was with the trumps and, consequently, discarded a spade on the ♣K. But Hamman ruffed and the contract went one down.

It should, perhaps, be mentioned here that Hamman and Lawrence were members of the United States' team that won the world championship in 1970 after the Italian 'blue' team had withdrawn. They were, it will be remembered, first called 'The Dallas Aces'. Later they became 'The USAces' and following further brilliant successes simply 'The Aces'. The other members of the original 'Aces' were James Jacoby, Robert Wolff, William Eisenberg and Robert Goldman.

Solution Number 8

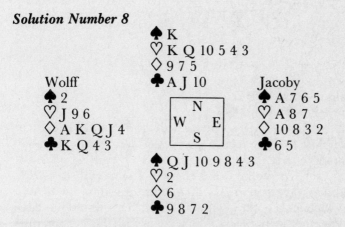

World Championships, Final, in Stockholm, 1970.
Contract: 3 ♠ doubled. Lead ◇K.
Robert Wolff switched to the ♣K which declarer took with dummy's ace and immediately laid down the ♠K. James Jacoby won with the ♠A, and hastened to play his last club and save the ruff, setting the contract, but the defence had not been imaginative enough — if it *had* been, the club lead should have been made to the first trick and thus saving West's diamond entry. In the circumstances declarer could have broken communication by ducking the first club and finessing the next one.

Then there would have been no ruff and declarer should have had time to establish the ♡Q and to discard his last club.

In the closed room Taiwan bid 5◊ with the result that William Eisenberg and Robert Goldman, too, became defenders. Eisenberg led a trump, but in any event declarer could not avoid the ♣A and two heart tricks, thus going down one.

Solution Number 9

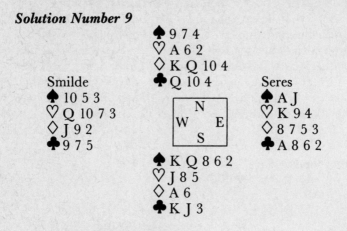

```
                    ♠ 9 7 4
                    ♡ A 6 2
                    ◊ K Q 10 4
    Smilde          ♣ Q 10 4          Seres
    ♠ 10 5 3                          ♠ A J
    ♡ Q 10 7 3        N              ♡ K 9 4
    ◊ J 9 2       W       E          ◊ 8 7 5 3
    ♣ 9 7 5           S              ♣ A 8 6 2
                    ♠ K Q 8 6 2
                    ♡ J 8 5
                    ◊ A 6
                    ♣ K J 3
```

Australia, Summer 1975.
    Contract: 4 ♠. Lead ♣9

Tim Seres immediately went up with the ♣A and, believe it or not, switched to the ♡K! Of course, declarer was deliberately led to believe that Seres also held the ♡Q. And so, with the ♡J in secret reserve he quite cheerfully won with dummy's ace and saw no reason to play diamonds three times to throw a heart, which looked like a winner. Moreover it would not have been altogether without risk if East got in with the ♣A and then played a fourth round of diamonds. In point of fact it would appear to be more reasonable to play trumps at once, and declarer did just that. Tim Seres won the ace at once and continued in hearts; the very much surprised declarer had to see Roelof Smilde win two hearts and then continue with the thirteenth heart. Seres ruffed with the ♠J and this uppercut assured a trump trick for Smilde, with the result that the contract went one down.

◊

22

Deal Number 10

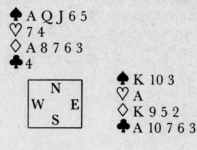

♠ A Q J 6 5
♡ 7 4
◇ A 8 7 6 3
♣ 4

♠ K 10 3
♡ A
◇ K 9 5 2
♣ A 10 7 6 3

North/Both.
The bidding:

North	South
1 ♠	2 ♡
3 ◇	3 ♡
3 ♠	3 NT

West leads the ♣9. How does East plan the defence?

Deal Number 11

♠ K J
♡ 10 7 4
◇ A 8 6
♣ A K J 6 2

♠ A 10 4
♡ Q 9 6 2
◇ K 7 2
♣ 8 4 3

North/Both.
The bidding:

North	South
1 ♣	1 NT
2 NT	3 NT

West leads the ♠5. Declarer goes up with dummy's ♠K and East wins with the ♠A. What does East lead?

Deal Number 12

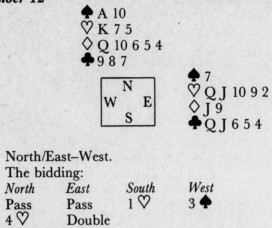

♠ A 10
♡ K 7 5
◇ Q 10 6 5 4
♣ 9 8 7

♠ 7
♡ Q J 10 9 2
◇ J 9
♣ Q J 6 5 4

North/East–West.
The bidding:

North	East	South	West
Pass	Pass	1 ♡	3 ♠
4 ♡	Double		

West leads the ♣Q. Declarer wins with the ♣K, draws the ♡A and continues with the ♡4 to dummy's king. Then the ◇4 to the ◇A in the closed hand and the ◇3. West wins with the ◇K and leads the ♠J. How does East continue?

Solution Number 10

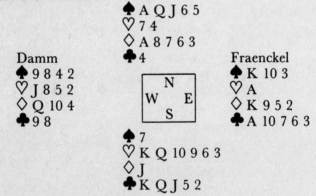

♠ A Q J 6 5
♡ 7 4
◇ A 8 7 6 3
♣ 4

Damm
♠ 9 8 4 2
♡ J 8 5 2
◇ Q 10 4
♣ 9 8

Fraenckel
♠ K 10 3
♡ A
◇ K 9 5 2
♣ A 10 7 6 3

♠ 7
♡ K Q 10 9 6 3
◇ J
♣ K Q J 5 2

Championship Open Pairs, Copenhagen, 1960.
    Contract: 3 No Trumps. Lead ♣9.
    Rigmor Fraenckel, suspecting a hidden club suit in South, went up with the ♣A and switched to the — ◇K! Thus she reduced dummy's total tricks to two!

Declarer won with dummy's ace and led the ♡4. East won and continued with the ◇2. Otti Damm cashed her two diamonds and switched to the ♣2. Declarer won with dummy's ace and played the ♡7, but could only take a total of seven tricks and thus went down two.

Solution Number 11

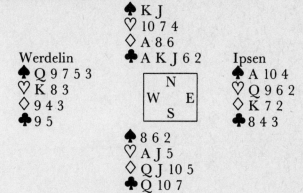

                    ♠ K J
                    ♡ 10 7 4
                    ◇ A 8 6
                    ♣ A K J 6 2
Werdelin   Ipsen
♠ Q 9 7 5 3   ♠ A 10 4
♡ K 8 3   N   ♡ Q 9 6 2
◇ 9 4 3   W   E   ◇ K 7 2
♣ 9 5   S   ♣ 8 4 3
                    ♠ 8 6 2
                    ♡ A J 5
                    ◇ Q J 10 5
                    ♣ Q 10 7

Trials in Copenhagen for the European Championships in Athens, 1971.

Contract: 3 No Trumps. Lead ♠5.

Declarer made the wrong decision when he went up with dummy's ♠K, as Thor Ipsen won with the ♠A. Partly to prevent the eventual ♠9 stopping the suit, and partly to be on lead after the third spade round, he continued with the ♠4. Stig Werdelin won with the ♠Q and returned the ♠3 to Ipsen's ♠10. Then Ipsen switched to the ♡2.

This was an unpleasant situation for declarer. He did not wish to let West in to his two good spades, particularly not if he could make the contract by finding West with the ◇K. So he went up with the ♡A and tried the diamond finesse. And then, of course, everything went wrong. Ipsen won and led the ♡6. Werdelin took the ♡K and his two good spades, and with Ipsen's additional two hearts the contract went down five.

In the closed room North became declarer at 3 No Trumps and got a heart lead. He covered with dummy's ♡J so that he might tempt West to continue in hearts. By doing this he avoided the spade guess and could finesse in diamonds. However, with the $\Diamond$K off-side he went down one. He *could* have made the contract if he had saved the $\heartsuit$J, always providing that he had made the correct guess on the expected spade switch, and finessed in hearts instead of diamonds.

Solution Number 12

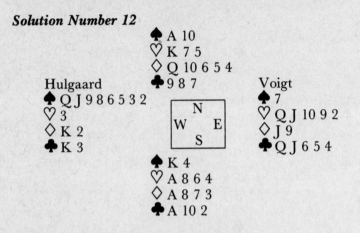

Hulgaard
♠ Q J 9 8 6 5 3 2
♡ 3
♢ K 2
♣ K 3

Voigt
♠ 7
♡ Q J 10 9 2
♢ J 9
♣ Q J 6 5 4

North:
♠ A 10
♡ K 7 5
♢ Q 10 6 5 4
♣ 9 8 7

South:
♠ K 4
♡ A 8 6 4
♢ A 8 7 3
♣ A 10 2

Pairs Olympiad at Amsterdam, 1966.
Contract: 4 $\heartsuit$ doubled. Lead ♣Q.

In this deal the Danes Axel Voigt and Johs. Hulgaard met the future world champions, Cornelius Slavenburg and Hans Kreijns of Holland; but, in the event, it was not this particular deal which assisted the latter pair towards their ultimate triumph.

Kreijns won the lead with the ♠K, cashed the $\heartsuit$A and led the $\heartsuit$4 to dummy's king. Then he led the $\Diamond$4 to the ace and another diamond. Hulgaard won with the $\Diamond$K and led the ♠J. Voigt ruffed and drew dummy's last trump, whereupon he switched to the ♣Q.

Declarer went up with the ♣A and continued in diamonds, but Voigt ducked until the fourth diamond, which he ruffed. Thus declarer got no discard, but had instead to give away two more tricks, and so went down three.

Deal Number 13

♠ 10 9
♡ K 8 7 6 4
◊ A K J 7 6 2
♣ —

```
      N
   W     E
      S
```

South/Both.
The bidding:

South	West	North	East
2 ♠	3 ◊	3 ♠	Pass
4 ♣	Pass	4 ♡	Pass
4 ♠	Pass	5 ♣	Pass
6 ♠			

What does West lead?

Deal Number 14

♠ A 5 4 3
♡ A J 3
◊ 10 6
♣ K Q J 2

♠ 9 6
♡ K 10 8 5
◊ K Q 4 2
♣ A 10 3

```
      N
   W     E
      S
```

West/North–South.
The bidding:

West	North	East	South
1 NT	Double	2 ◊	2 ♡

West leads the ◊K and continues with the queen which East takes over to switch to the ♣9. West goes up with the ♣A and continues with the ♣3. Declarer wins in dummy and plays a spade to the king in the closed hand in order to lead a trump. He finesses with the ♡J, draws the ace and continues with the ♡3. How has West planned the defence?

27

Deal Number 15

```
          ♠ J 8 6
          ♡ 4 3 2
          ◇ J 7 6
          ♣ K Q J 2
♠ A
♡ Q 10 8 5        N
◇ Q 10 8 3    W       E
♣ A 10 8 3        S
```

North/None.
The bidding:

North	East	South
Pass	Pass	4♠

West leads the ♡5. East wins with the ♡K and switches to the ◇9. Declarer wins with the ace and plays the ♣9. How does West plan the defence?

Solution Number 13

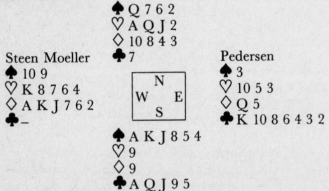

```
              ♠ Q 7 6 2
              ♡ A Q J 2
              ◇ 10 8 4 3
Steen Moeller ♣ 7              Pedersen
♠ 10 9                         ♠ 3
♡ K 8 7 6 4       N            ♡ 10 5 3
◇ A K J 7 6 2  W     E         ◇ Q 5
♣ –               S            ♣ K 10 8 6 4 3 2
              ♠ A K J 8 5 4
              ♡ 9
              ◇ 9
              ♣ A Q J 9 5
```

European Championships in Oslo, July 1968. Denmark-Turkey.
Contract: 6♠.

In a desperate attempt to get partner on lead Steffen Steen Moeller led the ◇2!

And it was successful. Arne Pedersen was greatly surprised, but quickly grasped the situation when he took the trick with the ◊Q. He then switched to a club which Steen ruffed — and the contract was one down.

To underlead top honours under similar circumstances is by no means unusual and has been done by others, including the following: Pierre Jaïs, France, in 1957 and in the European Championships 1973.
Pierre Forquet, Italy, in the World Championships, Como, 1958.
A. H. Woods-May Belle Long in the American Ladies' Championships, 1961.
Alvin Blinder in an American Duplicate, 1962.
Izhak Elenberg in the Olympiad 1964, Israel-Jamaica.
Stephen Robinson in a Duplicate at Chicago, 1965.
Théodore Caralli in a French Goulash-Bridge, 1972.

Solution Number 14

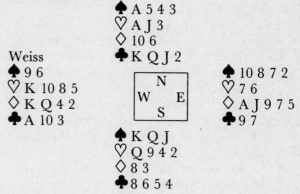

```
                    ♠ A 5 4 3
                    ♡ A J 3
                    ◊ 10 6
    Weiss           ♣ K Q J 2
    ♠ 9 6                              ♠ 10 8 7 2
    ♡ K 10 8 5          N             ♡ 7 6
    ◊ K Q 4 2       W       E         ◊ A J 9 7 5
    ♣ A 10 3           S              ♣ 9 7
                    ♠ K Q J
                    ♡ Q 9 4 2
                    ◊ 8 3
                    ♣ 8 6 5 4
```

Mixed-Pairs Olympiad, Las Palmas, May 1974.
Contract: 2♡. Lead ◊K.
After the ◊K and partner's 'come-on' Larry Weiss continued with the ◊Q which East took over to switch to the ♣9. Weiss went up with the ace and continued with the ♣3 to dummy's jack. Declarer played a spade to the king in the closed hand in order to take the trump finesse with the ♡J and draw the ♡A. Then Larry Weiss dropped the ♡10! This made declarer believe in a 3–3 distribution and so he continued with the ♡3. Weiss took the ♡9 with the king and forced declarer with a diamond, and as a result the ♡8 and another diamond set the contract.

Solution Number 15

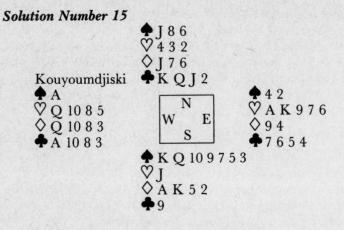

♠ J 8 6
♥ 4 3 2
♦ J 7 6
♣ K Q J 2

Kouyoumdjiski
♠ A
♥ Q 10 8 5
♦ Q 10 8 3
♣ A 10 8 3

♠ 4 2
♥ A K 9 7 6
♦ 9 4
♣ 7 6 5 4

♠ K Q 10 9 7 5 3
♥ J
♦ A K 5 2
♣ 9

I do not know the nationality of the man with so many vowels in his name, but in any case the hand was played in Belgium.

Contract: 4♠. Lead ♥5.

East won with the ♥K and then switched to the ♦9. Declarer won with the ♦A and hastened to lead the ♣9. With as much haste Mr K won with the ♣A and then led the ♦Q! It should be noted that if he had led a low diamond dummy would have won with the ♦J, and declarer would have thrown his last two diamonds on dummy's clubs before he played trumps. But he had to win the ♦Q with the king, and when he played trumps West came in on the ace in time to give East a diamond ruff to set the contract.

However, taking everything into account declarer's play should have been better, for East had shown the ♥A and K without having opened the bidding. Consequently it was highly probable that West would be holding the other two aces and declarer should, therefore, have at once played trumps. If West should then switch to a low diamond, dummy would win or the ♦Q would be taken with the king. East's last trump would have been drawn before the clubs were touched and when West won with the ♣A he could cause no more trouble.

Deal Number 16

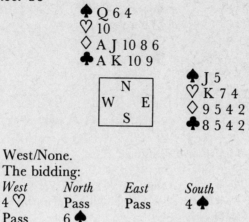

♠ Q 6 4
♡ 10
◇ A J 10 8 6
♣ A K 10 9

♠ J 5
♡ K 7 4
◇ 9 5 4 2
♣ 8 5 4 2

West/None.
The bidding:

West	North	East	South
4 ♡	Pass	Pass	4 ♠
Pass	6 ♠		

West leads the ♡A. What card does East play?

Deal Number 17

♠ Q 10 8 2
♡ A Q 4
◇ A 9 7
♣ A K 5

♠ J 6 4 3
♡ K 10 8
◇ J 10 6 3 2
♣ 7

North/Both.
The bidding:

North	South
1 ◇	1 NT
3 NT	

West leads the ◇3. East wins the trick with the ◇K and continues with the ◇8 to declarer's queen. The ♡2 is played to dummy's queen and the ♣2 to the ♣9 in the closed hand. West wins with the ♣J and continues in diamonds. Declarer wins with dummy's ace, draws the ♡A and continues with the ♡4. How has West planned the defence?

Deal Number 18

♠ A 9 7 6
♡ A Q 6 2
◇ Q 2
♣ Q 8 3

♠ K 5 2
♡ 8 7 5 4
◇ A 10 8
♣ K J 9

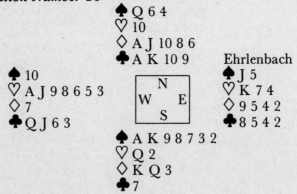

East/North–South.
The bidding:

East	South	West	North
Pass	Pass	1 NT	Double
ReDouble	2 ◇		

West leads the ♡8. Declarer finesses in dummy. East wins with the ♡K and switches to the ◇4, taken by West with the ace. What does West lead now?

Solution Number 16

♠ Q 6 4
♡ 10
◇ A J 10 8 6
♣ A K 10 9

Ehrlenbach

♠ 10
♡ A J 9 8 6 5 3
◇ 7
♣ Q J 6 3

♠ J 5
♡ K 7 4
◇ 9 5 4 2
♣ 8 5 4 2

♠ A K 9 8 7 3 2
♡ Q 2
◇ K Q 3
♣ 7

American Duplicate, 1955.
Contract: 6♠. Lead ♡A.
Jack Ehrlenbach dropped the ♡K!
West continued with a low heart, and for safety's sake declarer ruffed with dummy's ♠Q. Then when he saw East

32

follow with the ♡4 he was in a quandary as to its meaning — it could scarcely be a suit shift signal to diamonds. It seemed more probable that the basic idea was to manoeuvre declarer into ruffing high. If so this would mean that East held the ♠J–10–5. When, therefore, declarer led the ♣4 from dummy and Ehrlenbach followed with the ♣5 declarer finessed with the ♣7, and so West took the undertrick with his blank ♣10.

Solution Number 17

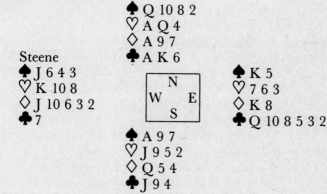

Steene

	♠ Q 10 8 2	
	♡ A Q 4	
	◇ A 9 7	
	♣ A K 6	
♠ J 6 4 3		♠ K 5
♡ K 10 8		♡ 7 6 3
◇ J 10 6 3 2		◇ K 8
♣ 7		♣ Q 10 8 5 3 2
	♠ A 9 7	
	♡ J 9 5 2	
	◇ Q 5 4	
	♣ J 9 4	

European Junior Championships, Copenhagen, 1974. Belgium-Great Britain.

Contract: 3 No Trumps. Lead 3◇.

East won the first trick with the ◇K and continued with the ◇8 to declarer's queen. The ♡2 was played to dummy's queen and the ♣2 from dummy. Ivan van de Steene took declarer's ♣9 with the jack and continued with a diamond. Dummy's ace won, the ♡A was drawn — and van de Steene dropped the ♡K!

Declarer, who did not know the lucky spade distribution, could hardly be blamed for now taking the 'marked' heart finesse with the ♡9 — and West's ♡10 and two long diamonds secured the undertrick.

Solution Number 18

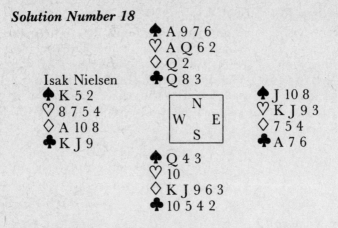

The Oslo Bowl, Norway, in the fifties.

Contract: 2◊. Lead ♡8.

Declarer finessed with dummy's ♡Q, and East won with the ♡K, to switch to the ◊4. Isak Nielsen (alias Sadar Sahib) won with the ◊A, and reasoning that East must be holding the ♣A for his redouble, Nielsen then led the ♣J and in this way the defenders secured three club tricks. With an exit in trumps a spade trick was unavoidable and so the contract went one down. Isak Nielsen himself admits that the contract almost certainly would have gone down in any case.

An almost similar defence was found by Ira Rubin in the Vanderbilt Tournament at Cleveland in 1969, the only difference being that he led the ♣10 from ♣K–10–2 in No Trumps, with ♣Q–x–x in dummy and ♣A–J–x–x with his partner; four tricks were therefore needed quickly.

A similar defence was made by Oscar Jormann, a Norwegian, somewhere about 1960, and here again it was a matter of four quick tricks, this time in spades.

Deal Number 19

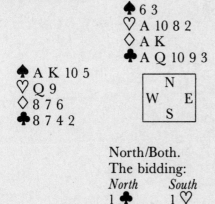

♠ K
♡ K J 10 8 6 4 3
◇ A Q J 3
♣ 8

♠ Q 8 6 4 3
♡ A 7 5
◇ 7 2
♣ Q 3 2

North/None.
The bidding:

North	South
1 ♣	1 ♡
2 ◇	4 NT
5 ♡	6 ◇

West leads the ♣4. Winning with dummy's king declarer leads the ♡8. East wins the trick with the ♡Q and switches to the ♣7. Declarer wins with the ace, draws two rounds of trumps and then the ♣K. How does West plan the defence from here?

Deal Number 20

♠ 6 3
♡ A 10 8 2
◇ A K
♣ A Q 10 9 3

♠ A K 10 5
♡ Q 9
◇ 8 7 6
♣ 8 7 4 2

North/Both.
The bidding:

North	South
1 ♣	1 ♡
4 ♡	

West cashes the two top spades and then leads the ♠5. East has followed with the ♠Q, 9 and J. Declarer ruffs with dummy's

♡2, draws the ♡A and lets the ♡10 run to West's ♡Q. What does West lead now?

Deal Number 21

♠ J 9 7 3 2
♡ A 8 5
◇ J 8 4
♣ 10 3

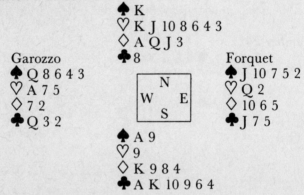

North/None.
The bidding:

North	South
2 NT	3 ♠
4 ♣	4 ◇
4 NT	5 ◇
6 ♣	6 ◇

What does West lead?

Solution Number 19

♠ K
♡ K J 10 8 6 4 3
◇ A Q J 3
♣ 8

Garozzo
♠ Q 8 6 4 3
♡ A 7 5
◇ 7 2
♣ Q 3 2

Forquet
♠ J 10 7 5 2
♡ Q 2
◇ 10 6 5
♣ J 7 5

♠ A 9
♡ 9
◇ K 9 8 4
♣ A K 10 9 6 4

Olympiad at Deauville, 1968. Italy-USA.
  Contract: 6◇. Lead ♣4.
  Winning with dummy's ♣K, declarer played the ♡8. This was where a beautiful defence started when Pietro Forquet, who felt intuitively that declarer did not hold the ♡A, went up with the ♡Q. He held the trick and then switched to the ♣7. Declarer won with the ♣A, drew two rounds of trumps and

then the ♣K. It was then that Benito Garozzo dropped the ♣Q. This completely fooled declarer and sidetracked him from his plan, incidentally the correct one, to set up the clubs by a single ruff. So, believing East to hold four clubs to the jack, he thought if he should ruff two clubs and ruff himself home twice he still could not draw the last trump. Instead, he drew it by a trump to dummy so as to play the ♡K and to let it run when Forquet followed with ♡2. By winning earlier with the ♡Q Forquet had led declarer to believe that he was also holding the ace. But, in the event, it was Garozzo who won with the ♡A, and the contract went down one.

Solution Number 20

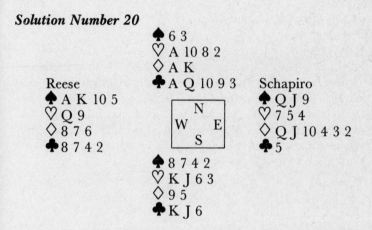

```
                    ♠ 6 3
                    ♡ A 10 8 2
                    ◇ A K
                    ♣ A Q 10 9 3
Reese                                   Schapiro
♠ A K 10 5                              ♠ Q J 9
♡ Q 9               ┌─────────┐        ♡ 7 5 4
◇ 8 7 6            │    N    │        ◇ Q J 10 4 3 2
♣ 8 7 4 2          │ W     E │        ♣ 5
                    │    S    │
                    └─────────┘
                    ♠ 8 7 4 2
                    ♡ K J 6 3
                    ◇ 9 5
                    ♣ K J 6
```

Olympiad in New York, 1964, 15th round, Great Britain-Italy.
Contract: 4♡. Lead ♠K.

Terence Reese continued in spades, dummy ruffing the third round with the ♡2. Declarer cashed dummy's ♡A and let the ♡10 run to West's ♡Q. This could scarcely be criticized because if a trump trick must be lost it is better to lose it while dummy's last trump protects the spades.

When Reese now played the ♣10 declarer was happy to ruff with dummy's ♡8. But the spade lead enabled Boris Schapiro to get rid of his singleton club, and when declarer tried to get to the closed hand in clubs Schapiro ruffed, and the contract went down one.

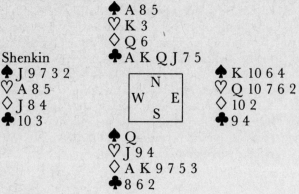

♠ A 8 5
♡ K 3
◇ Q 6
♣ A K Q J 7 5

Shenkin
♠ J 9 7 3 2
♡ A 8 5
◇ J 8 4
♣ 10 3

♠ K 10 6 4
♡ Q 10 7 6 2
◇ 10 2
♣ 9 4

♠ Q
♡ J 9 4
◇ A K 9 7 5 3
♣ 8 6 2

Pairs Olympiad at Las Palmas, 1974.
  Contract: 6◇.
  The young Scottish player Barnet Shenkin led the ♡5!
  The underlead of an ace against a slam is an unexpected lightening attack and may be the best chance if the distribution favours it. This time it succeeded. Declarer did not dream that Shenkin could have the ace, but he hoped that Shenkin would have the queen and he therefore played the ♡3 from dummy. East won the trick with the ♡Q and returned, of course, a heart so that the contract went one down.

Deal Number 22

♠ A K Q 6 5 3
♡ 10 6
♢ 4
♣ Q J 5 2

```
        N
    W       E
        S
```

♠ 8 7
♡ 5
♢ Q 9 8 7 3
♣ 10 9 8 7 3

East/North–South.
The bidding:

East	South	West	North
Pass	Pass	1 ♡	1 ♠
Pass	1 NT	2 ♡	3 ♣
Pass	3 NT		

West leads the ♢K. How does East plan the defence?

Deal Number 23

♠ Q 10 9 8
♡ 10 9 3 2
♢ Q 5 3
♣ J 9

♠ K J 7 5 2
♡ J 4
♢ 8
♣ K 8 6 3 2

```
        N
    W       E
        S
```

North/North–South.
The bidding:

North	East	South	West
Pass	Pass	1 ♡	1 ♠
2 ♡	2 ♠	4 ♡	4 ♠
5 ♡			

West leads the ♠5. Declarer ruffs East's ♠A with the ♡5 and enters dummy on the ♢Q to play the ♣9 to the queen in the closed hand. How does West plan the defence now and later?

39

Deal Number 24

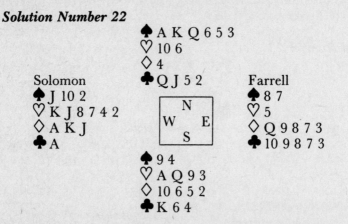

♠ 10 8 3
♡ 9 8
♢ K Q 8 6 3
♣ A 7 6

♠ K 7 4
♡ 6 5 4 2
♢ 9 2
♣ Q J 10 8

South/East–West.
The bidding:

South	North
1 NT	3 NT

West opens with the ♠Q and continues with the ♠5 to East's king which also holds the trick. What now?

Solution Number 22

♠ A K Q 6 5 3
♡ 10 6
♢ 4
♣ Q J 5 2

Solomon
♠ J 10 2
♡ K J 8 7 4 2
♢ A K J
♣ A

Farrell
♠ 8 7
♡ 5
♢ Q 9 8 7 3
♣ 10 9 8 7 3

♠ 9 4
♡ A Q 9 3
♢ 10 6 5 2
♣ K 6 4

Ladies' Pairs' Olympiad, 1966.

Contract: 3 No Trumps. Lead ♢K.

Mary Jane Farrell signalled to 'come-on' with the ♢9. Peggy Solomon continued with the ♢A and J, and even if Mary Jane thereby set up a diamond trick for declarer she took the jack over with the queen in order to be able to switch to hearts from the right side. Including the diamond trick declarer could now take no more than eight tricks, and went one down.

Solution Number 23

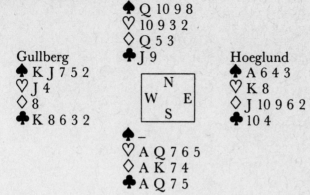

♠ Q 10 9 8
♡ 10 9 3 2
◇ Q 5 3
♣ J 9

Gullberg
♠ K J 7 5 2
♡ J 4
◇ 8
♣ K 8 6 3 2

```
      N
   W     E
      S
```

Hoeglund
♠ A 6 4 3
♡ K 8
◇ J 10 9 6 2
♣ 10 4

♠ —
♡ A Q 7 6 5
◇ A K 7 4
♣ A Q 7 5

Swedish Pairs Championships in Stockholm, April 1971.
   Contract: 5♡. Lead ♠5.
   South was concerned that the sacrifice might have been too cheap for he, himself, expected that he would be able to make five odd. In point of fact six odd were 'on ice' by leading a low club up to the jack. However, declarer chose to finesse both hearts and clubs. He ruffed East's ♠A and then led a diamond to dummy's queen to try the club finesse. Gullberg took the ♣Q with the king and exited with a club to dummy's jack. Then declarer tried the ♡2 to the queen and, so far, was lucky—but Gullberg followed with the ♡J! Declarer thought it likely that East had two hearts left and so tried to get into dummy by ruffing a low club; but Hoeglund overruffed with the ♡K and switched to a diamond which Gullberg ruffed, and the contract went one down.
   With such splendid play throughout the championship Gullberg-Hoeglund proved deserved and worthy winners.

Solution Number 24

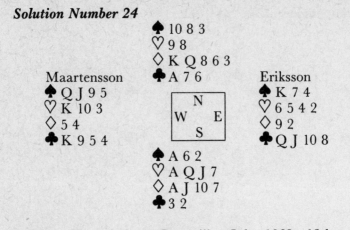

```
                      ♠ 10 8 3
                      ♡ 9 8
                      ◇ K Q 8 6 3
    Maartensson       ♣ A 7 6          Eriksson
    ♠ Q J 9 5          ┌─────────┐     ♠ K 7 4
    ♡ K 10 3           │    N    │     ♡ 6 5 4 2
    ◇ 5 4            W │ W     E │ E   ◇ 9 2
    ♣ K 9 5 4          │    S    │     ♣ Q J 10 8
                       └─────────┘
                      ♠ A 6 2
                      ♡ A Q J 7
                      ◇ A J 10 7
                      ♣ 3 2
```

Ladies' Olympiad at Deauville, July 1968, 12th round, Sweden-USA.

Contract: 3 No Trumps. Lead ♠Q.

Karin Eriksson followed with the ♠7 so Eva Maartensson continued with the ♠5, and the ♠K also held the trick.

The defence on this hand is run of the mill and clearly shows how declarer should *not* have played. With two spade tricks home and dry it could be understood that Mrs Eriksson thought these to be sufficient and so switched to the ♣Q. As a result declarer could now cash only five diamond tricks and three aces, so she tried to get the ninth trick with a heart finesse. The result was that the defenders then won three club tricks in addition to the ♡K, and the contract went down two.

With the favourable spade distribution declarer could have made the contract by winning the first spade trick and then establishing hearts. The second spade would be too late had the defenders switched immediately to clubs.

Deal Number 25

```
                    ♠ 2
                    ♡ J 10 6 3
                    ◇ K 10 6 3
                    ♣ J 10 7 5
                                    ♠ 6 5 4 3
                    ┌─────────┐     ♡ A 8 5
                    │    N    │     ◇ A J 9
                    │ W     E │     ♣ A 6 2
                    │    S    │
                    └─────────┘
```

South/Both.
The bidding:

South	North
2 NT	3 ♣
3 NT	

West leads the ♣J. Declarer wins with the ace and plays the
♡K. How does East plan the defence?

Deal Number 26

```
                    ♠ Q 9 8 2
                    ♡ A J 3
                    ◇ A 5
                    ♣ A J 9 3
  ♠ K 6
  ♡ 9 4 2          ┌─────────┐
  ◇ K Q J          │    N    │
  ♣ 10 8 6 5 2     │ W     E │
                   │    S    │
                   └─────────┘
```

North/Both.
The bidding:

North	South
1 ♣	1 NT
3 NT	

West leads the ♣5. Declarer wins with the ♣Q and plays a low
spade. How does West plan the defence?

Deal Number 27

                    ♠ 9 8
                    ♡ K 9
                    ◇ J 9 6 3 2
                    ♣ K Q J 9

                                    ♠ 10 4
                         N   ♡ A Q J 7 3
                    W   E   ◇ 8 7 5
                         S   ♣ A 4 3

West/North–South.
The bidding:

West	North	East	South
Pass	Pass	Pass	1 ♠
Pass	1 NT	2 ♡	3 ♠
Pass	4 ♠		

West leads the ♡6 and dummy covers with the ♡9. How should East plan the defence now and later?

Solution Number 25

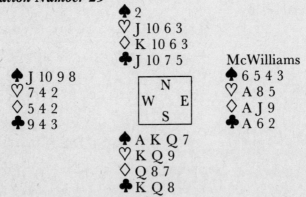

                    ♠ 2
                    ♡ J 10 6 3
                    ◇ K 10 6 3
                    ♣ J 10 7 5   McWilliams
    ♠ J 10 9 8   ♠ 6 5 4 3
    ♡ 7 4 2   N   ♡ A 8 5
    ◇ 5 4 2   W   E   ◇ A J 9
    ♣ 9 4 3   S   ♣ A 6 2
                    ♠ A K Q 7
                    ♡ K Q 9
                    ◇ Q 8 7
                    ♣ K Q 8

American Teams-of-four, 1966.
   Contract: 3 No Trumps. Lead ♣J.
   Declarer won with the ♣A and played in due course the ♡K and Q, the ♣K and Q and the ◇Q. Bill McWilliams ducked all five times!

After which it was impossible for declarer to get a single trick in dummy, and he won only eight tricks.

If East had won only one of declarer's honour cards, then declarer would have set up an entry into dummy for his ninth trick.

Solution Number 26

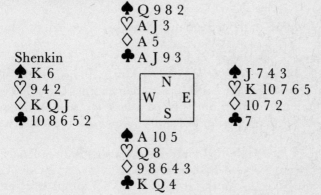

```
                    ♠ Q 9 8 2
                    ♡ A J 3
                    ◇ A 5
                    ♣ A J 9 3
Shenkin                             ♠ J 7 4 3
♠ K 6               ┌─────────┐     ♡ K 10 7 6 5
♡ 9 4 2             │    N    │     ◇ 10 7 2
◇ K Q J             │ W     E │     ♣ 7
♣ 10 8 6 5 2        │    S    │
                    └─────────┘
                    ♠ A 10 5
                    ♡ Q 8
                    ◇ 9 8 6 4 3
                    ♣ K Q 4
```

European Junior Championships in Copenhagen, 1974, Great Britain-Eire.

Contract: 3 No Trumps. Lead ♣5.

Declarer won with the ♣Q and played the ♠5. Barnet Shenkin, the young Scottish player in the British team, boldly followed with the ♠6! Declarer finessed with dummy's ♠8, and East won the trick with the ♠J. East switched to the ◇2. Dummy won with the ace and continued with the ◇5. Barnet won with the ◇Q and now switched to the ♡9 which ran to East's king. East now played the ♠3 and declarer, who still missed a trick, finessed again. Barnet cashed his blank king and took the undertrick with the ◇K.

At the other table Great Britain made the same contract by a double spade finesse.

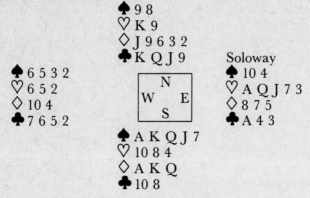

```
            ♠ 9 8
            ♡ K 9
            ◊ J 9 6 3 2
            ♣ K Q J 9          Soloway
♠ 6 5 3 2                      ♠ 10 4
♡ 6 5 2        ┌─────────┐     ♡ A Q J 7 3
◊ 10 4         │    N    │     ◊ 8 7 5
♣ 7 6 5 2      │  W   E  │     ♣ A 4 3
               │    S    │
               └─────────┘
            ♠ A K Q J 7
            ♡ 10 8 4
            ◊ A K Q
            ♣ 10 8
```

The Vanderbilt Tournament, Final, at Cleveland, March 1969.

Contract: 4♠. Lead ♡6.

Paul Soloway won with the ♡J and switched to the ♠4! Declarer won and led the ♣10 and then another club. Soloway won the second club and played the ♠10, so dummy was blocked. Declarer had to lose two more heart tricks and went down one.

At the other table the contract was also 4♠ after East had opened with 2♡ and had been raised by West, incidentally frightening North–South away from 3 No Trumps which was cold on North's hand. But then East–West let declarer make the contract. West opened with the ♡6 and declarer followed with the ♡8 to East's jack. East who was left wondering on what West could have raised him, switched to a diamond, with the result that declarer won time to have his third heart ruffed.

It is of interest to mention here that Paul Soloway was invited to complete the USAces team for the 1972 Olympiad after William Eisenberg had withdrawn.

Deal Number 28

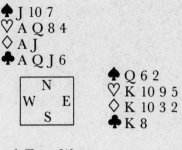

♠ J 10 7
♡ A Q 8 4
◇ A J
♣ A Q J 6

♠ Q 6 2
♡ K 10 9 5
◇ K 10 3 2
♣ K 8

North/East–West.
The bidding:

North	South
1 ♣	1 ♠
2 NT	3 ♠
4 ♠	

West leads the ♡2 and declarer finesses with dummy's queen. How does East plan the defence?

Deal Number 29

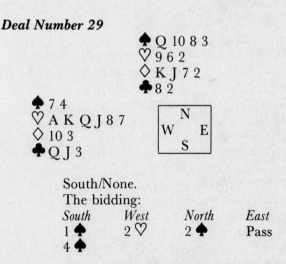

♠ Q 10 8 3
♡ 9 6 2
◇ K J 7 2
♣ 8 2

♠ 7 4
♡ A K Q J 8 7
◇ 10 3
♣ Q J 3

South/None.
The bidding:

South	West	North	East
1 ♠	2 ♡	2 ♠	Pass
4 ♠			

West leads the ♡K, East following with the ♡5 and South with the ♡4. What should West play next?

47

Deal Number 30

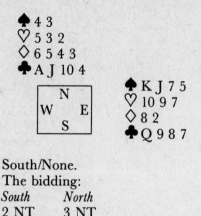

♠ 4 3
♡ 5 3 2
◇ 6 5 4 3
♣ A J 10 4

♠ K J 7 5
♡ 10 9 7
◇ 8 2
♣ Q 9 8 7

South/None.
The bidding:

South	North
2 NT	3 NT

West leads the ◇Q. Declarer cashes the ◇A and K and continues with the ◇10. But now you had better turn the page and look at both defenders' hands.

Solution Number 28

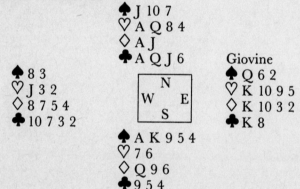

♠ J 10 7
♡ A Q 8 4
◇ A J
♣ A Q J 6

Giovine

♠ 8 3
♡ J 3 2
◇ 8 7 5 4
♣ 10 7 3 2

♠ Q 6 2
♡ K 10 9 5
◇ K 10 3 2
♣ K 8

♠ A K 9 5 4
♡ 7 6
◇ Q 9 6
♣ 9 5 4

Italian Duplicate, 1963.
Contract: 4♠. Lead ♡2.

Declarer finessed with dummy's ♡Q. Michele Giovine won with the king and switched to—the ♣8! He saw that his trump queen was in immediate danger of being finessed if he, unimaginatively, played the ♡10. Declarer was thus bamboozled into believing the ♣8 to be a singleton and, consequently, dared not risk letting West into lead by a failed trump finesse, so instead he drew in succession three trumps from the top. Winning the ♠Q Giovine exited with a heart. Later on declarer took the 'marked' club finesse, and as a diamond loser could not be avoided the contract went one down.

Solution Number 29

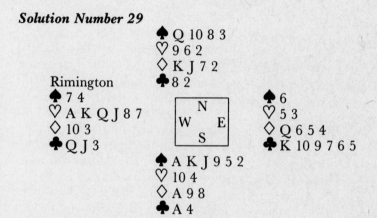

```
                        ♠ Q 10 8 3
                        ♡ 9 6 2
                        ◇ K J 7 2
        Rimington       ♣ 8 2
        ♠ 7 4                              ♠ 6
        ♡ A K Q J 8 7        N            ♡ 5 3
        ◇ 10 3          W        E        ◇ Q 6 5 4
        ♣ Q J 3             S            ♣ K 10 9 7 6 5
                        ♠ A K J 9 5 2
                        ♡ 10 4
                        ◇ A 9 8
                        ♣ A 4
```

Caransa Cup, Amsterdam, 1978.
  Contract: 4 ♠. Lead ♡K,
  At the other table West cashed another heart before switching to clubs, but declarer then eliminated hearts and trumps and endplayed the opponents in clubs.
  Derek Rimington had prevented this endplay by having already switched to the ♣Q in the second trick. When declarer, after drawing trumps, played a heart Rimington could cash the ♣J before exiting with a third heart. This, of course, is the 'Houdini Coup'. Declarer could, all the same, have made the contract by a backward diamond finesse; but instead he took the normal finesse, lost to East's ◇Q, and so went one down.

Solution Number 30

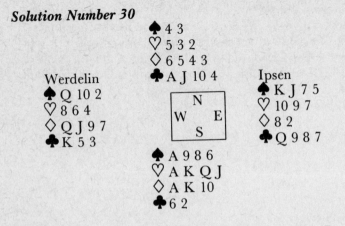

```
                        ♠ 4 3
                        ♡ 5 3 2
                        ◇ 6 5 4 3
                        ♣ A J 10 4
      Werdelin              N         Ipsen
      ♠ Q 10 2                        ♠ K J 7 5
      ♡ 8 6 4        W         E      ♡ 10 9 7
      ◇ Q J 9 7                       ◇ 8 2
      ♣ K 5 3              S          ♣ Q 9 8 7
                        ♠ A 9 8 6
                        ♡ A K Q J
                        ◇ A K 10
                        ♣ 6 2
```

European Championships in Athens, Greece, 1971. Denmark-Norway.

Contract: 3 No Trumps. Lead ◇Q.

Declarer won with the ◇A, cashed the ◇K and continued with the ◇10 to see whether the fourth diamond in dummy should become high. But Stig Werdelin won with the ◇J, cashed the ◇9 and switched, after Thor Ipsen's 'come-on' with the ♠7, to the ♠2. Declarer took the ♠K with the ace and ran his four high hearts. At this point Ipsen became a little embarrassed, but Werdelin made the way easier for him by jettisoning the ♣K. Ipsen thus needed to retain only two clubs, and when declarer exited in spades Ipsen took very good care to let Werdelin win the third spade so that clubs could come from the right side. The contract went down one.

Deal Number 31

```
                    ♠ A Q J 8
                    ♡ 10
                    ◇ K Q 6 4
                    ♣ A 10 7 6
   ♠ K 4           ┌─────────┐
   ♡ A K 8 3 2     │    N    │
   ◇ A 5           │ W     E │
   ♣ J 8 4 3       │    S    │
                    └─────────┘
```

West/Both.
The bidding:

West	North	East	South
1 ♡	Double	2 ♡	2 ♠
Pass	4 ♠		

West leads the ♡K, East following with the ♡4 and South with the ♡5. What does West lead next?

Deal Number 32

```
                    ♠ K 4 2
                    ♡ 8 4 2
                    ◇ A K 5
                    ♣ 10 9 4 3
   ♠ 8 7           ┌─────────┐
   ♡ A 10 9 5      │    N    │
   ◇ Q 7 3 2       │ W     E │
   ♣ K Q 6         │    S    │
                    └─────────┘
```

North/North–South.
The bidding:

North	South
Pass	1 NT
3 NT	

West leads the ♡5. Declarer takes East's ♡J with the king and plays the ♠3 to dummy's king to try the finesse with the ♣3 to the jack. West wins with the ♣K. What next?

Deal Number 33

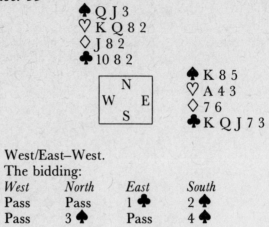

♠ Q J 3
♡ K Q 8 2
◇ J 8 2
♣ 10 8 2

♠ K 8 5
♡ A 4 3
◇ 7 6
♣ K Q J 7 3

West/East–West.
The bidding:

West	North	East	South
Pass	Pass	1 ♣	2 ♠
Pass	3 ♠	Pass	4 ♠

West leads the ♣5. Declarer takes East's ♣J with the ace and plays the ♡J. How does East plan the defence?

Solution Number 31

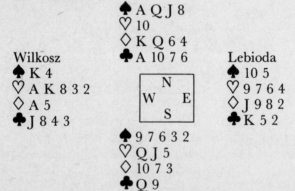

♠ A Q J 8
♡ 10
◇ K Q 6 4
♣ A 10 7 6

Wilkosz
♠ K 4
♡ A K 8 3 2
◇ A 5
♣ J 8 4 3

Lebioda
♠ 10 5
♡ 9 7 6 4
◇ J 9 8 2
♣ K 5 2

♠ 9 7 6 3 2
♡ Q J 5
◇ 10 7 3
♣ Q 9

Bridge Festival at Deauville, 1971. Poland (E-W)-Italy.
Contract: 4 ♠. Lead ♡K.

Andrzej Wilkosz thought that if declarer held the ♣K there could be no chance for the defence, but if Lebioda should be holding that card *and* the ◇J, declarer would then miss a quick entry to the closed hand. Thus there would be a possible

52

opening, and so he cashed the ♢A and continued with the ♢5. Declarer had to win with dummy's ♢Q, and if he now tried to come to the closed hand with a low club Lukasz Lebioda would go up with the king and lead a diamond. Therefore, declarer chose to try and find the ♠K singleton and played the ♣A—but he had to lose a trick to each of the black kings and consequently went down one.

Solution Number 32

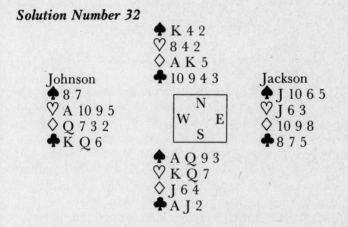

```
                    ♠ K 4 2
                    ♡ 8 4 2
                    ♢ A K 5
    Johnson         ♣ 10 9 4 3        Jackson
    ♠ 8 7                             ♠ J 10 6 5
    ♡ A 10 9 5           N            ♡ J 6 3
    ♢ Q 7 3 2       W       E         ♢ 10 9 8
    ♣ K Q 6             S             ♣ 8 7 5
                    ♠ A Q 9 3
                    ♡ K Q 7
                    ♢ J 6 4
                    ♣ A J 2
```

International Tournament at Dun Laoghaire, Eire, 1971.
    Contract: 3 No Trumps. Lead ♡5.
    Howard Jackson of Britain could put on only the ♡J which declarer took with the king. He then played the ♠3 to dummy's king to try the finesse of the ♣3 to the ♣J, which A. H. Johnson of Ireland won with the ♣K. In point of fact Johnson was already endplayed, but with the knowledge that declarer was afraid of letting East in to play hearts he led the ♢7. Declarer certainly considered ducking in dummy but, nevertheless, decided to go up with the king and to continue with the ♣10. Johnson won the ♣Q and was in the same position as previously, but on this occasion he found a lead which would give declarer an extra trick, but at the same time blocked dummy's fourth club—so he led the ♢Q! It was then impossible for declarer to get the ninth trick.

Solution Number 33

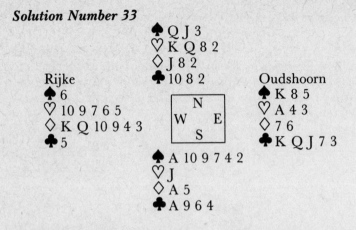

♠ Q J 3
♡ K Q 8 2
◇ J 8 2
♣ 10 8 2

Rijke
♠ 6
♡ 10 9 7 6 5
◇ K Q 10 9 4 3
♣ 5

Oudshoorn
♠ K 8 5
♡ A 4 3
◇ 7 6
♣ K Q J 7 3

♠ A 10 9 7 4 2
♡ J
◇ A 5
♣ A 9 6 4

Bridge Festival at Juan-les-Pins, 1963. Holland East-West.
   Contract: 4♠. Lead ♣5.
   Declarer took the ♣J with the ace and led the ♡J. With his lowest heart Rijke showed three or five, Leo Oudshoorn could see that it must be five since nothing accounted for declarer's lead of the jack from three hearts. Consequently Oudshoorn won with the ♡A and cashed the ♣Q. As Rijke threw the ◇10 Oudshoorn immediately switched to the ◇7. Thus declarer had to lose a diamond and another club trick before he could get into dummy to finesse trumps and thus went down one.
   But if East had cashed another club before the diamond switch declarer could have made the contract, for then he could have gone up on the ◇A, ruffed his last club (or overruffed West), discarded the ◇5 on the ♡K and led the ♠Q from dummy.

Deal Number 34

          ♠ K 9 6
          ♡ Q 5 4
          ◇ A 9 8 5
          ♣ Q 10 4

♠ 10 7 5 3
♡ K 9 7
◇ K J 6 3
♣ K 6

North/None.
The bidding:

North	South
Pass	2 ♡
2 NT	3 ♣
4 ♡	

The opening bid shows 10–15 high card points and at least a
five-card-suit. 2 No Trumps is forcing and 3 ♣ shows seven
black cards, unveiling a singleton or void in diamonds.
    West leads the ♠7. Dummy's king wins the trick, East
following with the ♣2. The ♡Q is played from dummy and
declarer ducks. What is West's plan?

Deal Number 35

          ♠ A K 7
          ♡ 6
          ◇ Q J 9 6 3
          ♣ K 8 4 3

                              ♠ 6 4 3 2
                              ♡ 10 9
                              ◇ K 10
                              ♣ A Q 9 5 2

South/East–West.
The bidding:

North	South
1 ♠	2 ◇
2 ♠	3 ♠
4 ◇	4 ♠

55

West leads the ♣J, dummy and East following with low clubs. Declarer ruffs with the ♠8 and draws the ♡A and ◇A. How does East judge the situation?

Deal Number 36

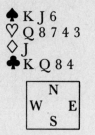

♠ K J 6
♡ Q 8 7 4 3
◇ J
♣ K Q 8 4

♠ 10 9 3
♡ J 10 9 6
◇ A K Q 4
♣ A J

South/North–South.
The bidding:

South	West	North	East
1 ♣	Pass	1 ♡	Double
Pass	1 ♠	2 ♣	Pass
2 NT	Pass	3 NT	

West leads the ◇2. How does East plan the defence?

Solution Number 34

♠ K 9 6
♡ Q 5 4
◇ A 9 8 5
♣ Q 10 4

Desrousseaux
♠ 10 7 5 3
♡ K 9 7
◇ K J 6 3
♣ K 6

Devriès
♠ J 8 2
♡ 8 2
◇ Q 10 7 4
♣ A 9 7 2

♠ A Q 4
♡ A J 10 6 3
◇ 2
♣ J 8 5 3

World Championships, Mixed-Pairs, Amsterdam, 1966.
  Contract: 4♡. Lead ♣7.
  Declarer won with dummy's ♣K, East following with the

56

♠2. The ♡Q was played from dummy and was allowed to run to Gérard Desrousseaux' king. He tried to reconstruct declarer's hand. With a singleton or void in diamonds already unveiled during the bidding and, furthermore, already marked with the ♠A, the ♡A-J and probably the ♠Q, there was hardly room for the ♣A within the point limit even if he held the maximum.

Desrousseaux therefore led the ♣K and continued with the ♣6. Madeleine Devriès took the second club trick and led a third club for partner to ruff so the contract went one down, giving the French pair 30 Match Points out of 34 possible.

Solution Number 35

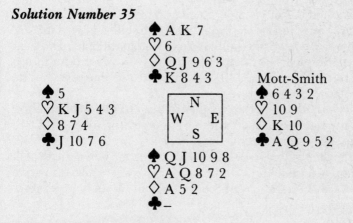

Rubber Bridge in USA, 1962.
Contract: 4 ♠. Lead ♣J.

Declarer ruffed with the ♠8 and cashed both the red aces. It was fairly clear that his plan was to cross-ruff the next six tricks and then take the tenth trick with his high trump. Geoffrey Mott-Smith suspected this and, as a red herring, dropped the ◇K under the ace. Declarer fell for it—the stakes were high and overtricks added up to a lot of dollars. And so declarer changed his intentions and drew four rounds of trumps, and took the 'marked' diamond finesse. Mott-Smith won with the ◇10, and declarer won no more tricks.

Solution Number 36

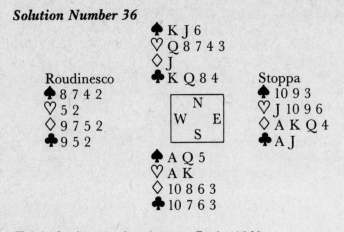

Roudinesco — ♠ 8 7 4 2 ♡ 5 2 ◇ 9 7 5 2 ♣ 9 5 2

Stoppa — ♠ 10 9 3 ♡ J 10 9 6 ◇ A K Q 4 ♣ A J

North — ♠ K J 6 ♡ Q 8 7 4 3 ◇ J ♣ K Q 8 4

South — ♠ A Q 5 ♡ A K ◇ 10 8 6 3 ♣ 10 7 6 3

Trials for international team, Paris, 1969.

Contract: 3 No Trumps. Lead ◇2.

Jean-Louis Stoppa won with the ◇K and then played the ◇4! Declarer, who understood that the opening lead had to be from four to the queen, finessed with the ◇8. Jean-Marc Roudinesco won the trick with the ◇9 and continued in that suit. So the contract went one down.

It was, indeed, declarer's misfortune that he held as big a spot card as the ◇8. With other, lower cards to the 10 there would have been nothing else to do but to go up with the ◇10, and then the clubs would have been tried, and when the ♣J fell in the second round, declarer would have had sufficient tricks. His other alternative would have been to try and see whether the hearts would break.

Deal Number 37

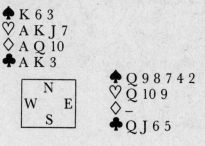

                    ♠ K 6 3
                    ♡ A K J 7
                    ◇ A Q 10
                    ♣ A K 3

                                        ♠ Q 9 8 7 4 2
        ┌─────────┐   ♡ Q 10 9
        │   N   │   ◇ –
        │ W   E │   ♣ Q J 6 5
        │   S   │
        └─────────┘

North/North–South.
The bidding:
North   *South*
2 ♡   2 NT
3 NT

West leads the ♠J. Declarer wins with dummy's king, East dropping the ♣9. The next trick is taken with dummy's ♡K. What card does East throw?

Deal Number 38

                    ♠ 5 4 2
                    ♡ K 5 3
                    ◇ A Q 8 7
                    ♣ J 5 2

                                        ♠ 10 6
        ┌─────────┐   ♡ 10 7 6 4 2
        │   N   │   ◇ K 5 2
        │ W   E │   ♣ Q 10 7
        │   S   │
        └─────────┘

South/Both.
The bidding:
South   *North*
1 ♣   1 ◇
2 NT   3 NT

West leads the ♡Q, holding the trick. East follows with the ♡7 and West continues with the ♡J. Declarer wins with the ace and plays the ◇J. East ducks and next comes the ◇10. How does East plan the defence?

Deal Number 39

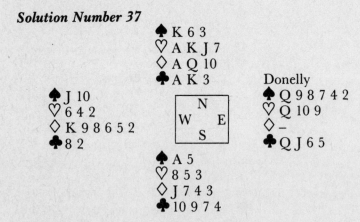

♠ 9 6 2
♡ A 9 7
◇ 8 5 2
♣ A K Q 5

♠ A K J 7
♡ –
◇ A Q 10 7 4 3
♣ 10 8 3

West/East–West.
The bidding:

West	North	East	South
1 ♠	Double	Pass	4 ♡

According to their system East must not pass to the double with less than three spades. West leads the ♠K and East follows with the ♠10 which thus cannot be a doubleton. How does West continue?

Solution Number 37

♠ K 6 3
♡ A K J 7
◇ A Q 10
♣ A K 3

Donelly

♠ J 10
♡ 6 4 2
◇ K 9 8 6 5 2
♣ 8 2

♠ Q 9 8 7 4 2
♡ Q 10 9
◇ –
♣ Q J 6 5

♠ A 5
♡ 8 5 3
◇ J 7 4 3
♣ 10 9 7 4

American Duplicate, 1967.
    Contract: 3 No Trumps. Lead ♠J.
    Declarer won with dummy's ♠K and played the ♡K. Jack Donelly dropped the ♡10 and, encouraged by this, declarer continued with the ♡A on which Donelly dropped the queen!

60

The intention, and it was a perfectly sound one, was to fool declarer into using his, very probably, sole entry to be able to finesse in hearts, and *not* in diamonds. Declarer swallowed what was dangled before him, for it looked to him as if hearts were set up with a finesse against West's ♡9; in any event he preferred what seemed to him a sure thing against a problematical diamond finesse. So he led a spade to the ace, played the ♡8 and let it run. Inevitably Donelly got his ♡9 and took four spades tricks, with the result—one down.

Solution Number 38

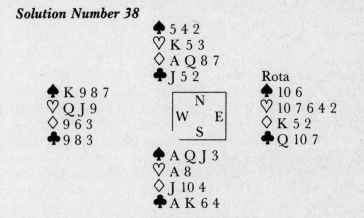

```
                    ♠ 5 4 2
                    ♡ K 5 3
                    ◇ A Q 8 7
                    ♣ J 5 2
                                        Rota
  ♠ K 9 8 7            ┌─────────┐      ♠ 10 6
  ♡ Q J 9          N   │         │      ♡ 10 7 6 4 2
  ◇ 9 6 3        W     │    E    │      ◇ K 5 2
  ♣ 9 8 3            S   │         │      ♣ Q 10 7
                      └─────────┘
                    ♠ A Q J 3
                    ♡ A 8
                    ◇ J 10 4
                    ♣ A K 6 4
```

International Tournament in Italy, 1960.

Contract: 3 No Trumps. Lead ♡Q.

West held the trick and followed on with the ♡J. Declarer won with the ♡A and then played the ◇J. East ducked, and declarer continued with the ◇10. In a brave attempt to block dummy Ottavio Rota ducked again. Now, declarer, an eminent French player, continued with the ◇4 and, after thinking a while, decided to finesse. So Rota got his blank king, but if there was to be any purpose in this defence he had to leave the hearts alone and switch to the ♠10. West took declarer's ♠J with the king and led the ♣9.

Declarer had no entry to the two tricks in dummy but had to lose a trick in each of the black suits and, consequently, went one down. He gave in too early—why didn't he cash two spades and then endplay East in clubs?

Solution Number 39

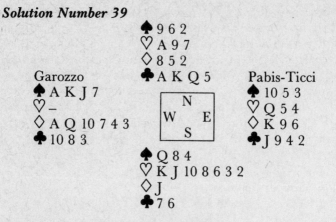

Tournament in Italy in the late sixties.

Contract: 4♡. Lead ♠K.

Pabis-Ticci followed with the ♠10. Although they did not usually play together Benito Garozzo and Camillo Pabis-Ticci were on this particular occasion partners and their bidding system did not allow Pabis-Ticci to pass 1♠ doubled if he had fewer than three of that suit. Consequently the ♠10 could not be a doubleton. Conceivably it could be the queen, but Garozzo felt that with the Q-10-x Pabis-Ticci would have tried to pre-empt. There must have been some reasoning and Garozzo came to the conclusion that it could only be a suit-preference signal. But to which diamond, the king or a singleton? Garozzo offered a short prayer to Saint Januarius, lit a cigarette which he thoughtfully smoked, and then eventually played a low diamond. Pabis-Ticci won with the ♢K and then played spades through the declarer's queen—and the contract went down one.

Deal Number 40

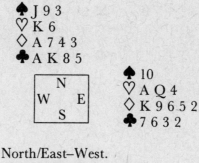

♠ J 9 3
♡ K 6
◇ A 7 4 3
♣ A K 8 5

♠ 10
♡ A Q 4
◇ K 9 6 5 2
♣ 7 6 3 2

North/East–West.
The bidding:

North	South
1 ◇	1 ♠
2 ♣	4 ♠

West leads the ♣Q. Declarer wins with dummy's king and ruffs the ♣5 in order to play the ♡3 to the king. How does East plan the defence?

Deal Number 41

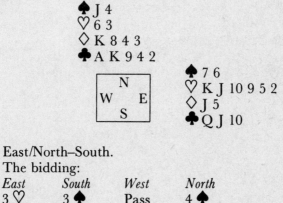

♠ J 4
♡ 6 3
◇ K 8 4 3
♣ A K 9 4 2

♠ 7 6
♡ K J 10 9 5 2
◇ J 5
♣ Q J 10

East/North–South.
The bidding:

East	South	West	North
3 ♡	3 ♠	Pass	4 ♠

West leads the ♡Q. How does East plan the defence?

Deal Number 42

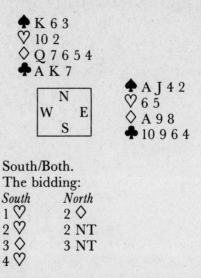

♠ K 6 3
♡ 10 2
◇ Q 7 6 5 4
♣ A K 7

♠ A J 4 2
♡ 6 5
◇ A 9 8
♣ 10 9 6 4

South/Both.
The bidding:

South	North
1 ♡	2 ◇
2 ♡	2 NT
3 ◇	3 NT
4 ♡	

West leads the ♠10. East lets it run to declarer's queen. A club is led to dummy's king in order to try the trump finesse. West wins with the ♡K and continues in spades. Declarer ruffs the third spade, draws trumps twice and plays the ◇3 to dummy's queen. How does East plan the defence from here?

Solution Number 40

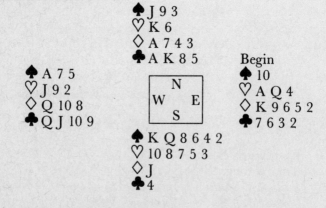

♠ J 9 3
♡ K 6
◇ A 7 4 3
♣ A K 8 5

Begin

♠ A 7 5
♡ J 9 2
◇ Q 10 8
♣ Q J 10 9

♠ 10
♡ A Q 4
◇ K 9 6 5 2
♣ 7 6 3 2

♠ K Q 8 6 4 2
♡ 10 8 7 5 3
◇ J
♣ 4

Canadian Championships, 1965.
    Contract: 4♠. Lead ♣Q.

64

Declarer won with dummy's ♣K, and ruffed the ♣5 in order to play the ♡3 to the king.

Jackie Begin won with the ace and switched to the ♠10. West went up on the ace and continued with a trump. Dummy won and played the ♡6 and Jackie Begin ducked! Having no more trumps herself she hoped that West could win the trick and remove dummy's last trump. This was exactly what happened, and the contract went one down.

Solution Number 41

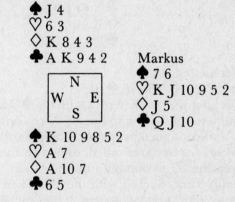

♠ J 4
♡ 6 3
♢ K 8 4 3
♣ A K 9 4 2

Markus
♠ 7 6
♡ K J 10 9 5 2
♢ J 5
♣ Q J 10

♠ A Q 3
♡ Q 8 4
♢ Q 9 6 2
♣ 8 7 3

♠ K 10 9 8 5 2
♡ A 7
♢ A 10 7
♣ 6 5

London, 1974.

Contract: 4 ♠. Lead ♡Q.

In an attempt to secure an entry Rixi Markus took the queen over with the king, but declarer won with the ace and played the ♣5 to dummy to play the ♠J, and let it run. West won with the ♣Q and continued in hearts, and Rixi won with the jack. Even although West's opening lead might have indicated a doubleton Mrs Markus switched to the ♢5. This was partly an attempt to set up a diamond trick for the defence, partly to block the club suit which otherwise could have been quickly set up. However, being interested in saving dummy's entry declarer won with the ♢A, but when winning the next trick with the ♠A West continued with the ♢2. Dummy's entry was made too early, and so the contract went one down.

It can be seen how important the playing of the ♢5 was and not the jack, for otherwise West would have been unable to continue in diamonds.

Solution Number 42

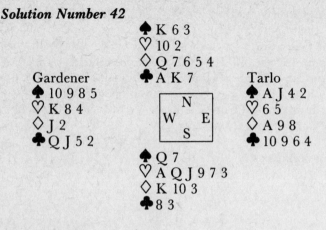

♠ K 6 3
♥ 10 2
♦ Q 7 6 5 4
♣ A K 7

Gardener
♠ 10 9 8 5
♥ K 8 4
♦ J 2
♣ Q J 5 2

Tarlo
♠ A J 4 2
♥ 6 5
♦ A 9 8
♣ 10 9 6 4

♠ Q 7
♥ A Q J 9 7 3
♦ K 10 3
♣ 8 3

London, 1960.
   Contract: 4♥. Lead ♠10.

Declarer won the first trick with the ♠Q and played a club to dummy to try the trump finesse. Nico Gardener won with the ♥K and continued in spades. Louis Tarlo won and played a third spade. Declarer ruffed, drew two rounds of trumps and played the ♦3 to dummy's queen.

Louis Tarlo ducked with the ♦8! Then came the ♦4 from dummy and Tarlo followed with the ♦9! Declarer was now led to believe that Gardener held the ♦A, and, hoping that Tarlo held the jack, declarer finessed the ♦10. Thus East-West won two diamond tricks, and the contract went one down.

Deal Number 43

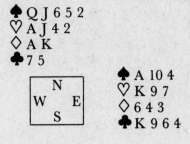

♠ Q J 6 5 2
♡ A J 4 2
◇ A K
♣ 7 5

♠ A 10 4
♡ K 9 7
◇ 6 4 3
♣ K 9 6 4

South/East–West.
The bidding:

South	North
2 ◇	2 NT
3 ♡	

West led the ♣A and continued with the ♣Q, ruffed by South who then led the ♡5 and finessed with dummy's jack. How should East plan the defence?

Deal Number 44

♠ K J 9 5
♡ 9 5 4
◇ K
♣ Q 9 8 7 4

♠ A 10 6 4
♡ A Q 10 7 2
◇ 9 8 7
♣ 6

North/North–South.
The bidding:

North	East	South	West
Pass	1 ◇	Pass	1 ♡
Double	2 ◇	2 ♠	Double

West leads the ◇9 and East takes dummy's king with the ace. East switches to the ♡J, declarer covers with the king and West cashes three heart tricks. What now?

67

Deal Number 45

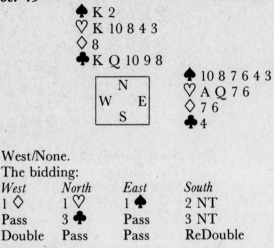

♠ K 2
♡ K 10 8 4 3
◇ 8
♣ K Q 10 9 8

♠ 10 8 7 6 4 3
♡ A Q 7 6
◇ 7 6
♣ 4

West/None.
The bidding:

West	North	East	South
1 ◇	1 ♡	1 ♠	2 NT
Pass	3 ♣	Pass	3 NT
Double	Pass	Pass	ReDouble

West leads the ♡J and declarer covers with dummy's king. how does East plan the defence?

Solution Number 43

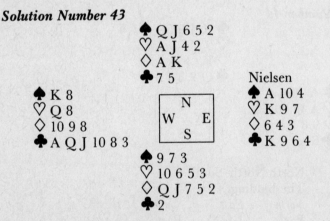

♠ Q J 6 5 2
♡ A J 4 2
◇ A K
♣ 7 5

Nielsen

♠ K 8
♡ Q 8
◇ 10 9 8
♣ A Q J 10 8 3

♠ A 10 4
♡ K 9 7
◇ 6 4 3
♣ K 9 6 4

♠ 9 7 3
♡ 10 6 5 3
◇ Q J 7 5 2
♣ 2

Duplicate, Copenhagen, March 1979.
    Contract: 3♡. Lead ♣A.
    The 2◇ bid was supposed to be the modern multi-coloured variety and proved to be the weak one—and very weak, indeed.

68

West led the ♣A and continued with the ♣Q which was ruffed by declarer. Hoping for at least one honour doubleton with West, declarer led the ♡3 and finessed with the ♡J. The distribution was what South could hope for, however Bertil L. Nielsen, winning with the ♡K, switched to the ♠4. West won with the ♠K, returned the ♠8, and on a third spade West scored the undertrick with the ♡Q.

Solution Number 44

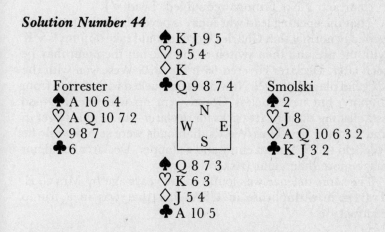

Forrester
♠ A 10 6 4
♡ A Q 10 7 2
♢ 9 8 7
♣ 6

♠ K J 9 5
♡ 9 5 4
♢ K
♣ Q 9 8 7 4

Smolski
♠ 2
♡ J 8
♢ A Q 10 6 3 2
♣ K J 3 2

♠ Q 8 7 3
♡ K 6 3
♢ J 5 4
♣ A 10 5

The Camrose Final, Great Britain, 1978.
  Contract: 2♠doubled. Lead: ♢9.
  Roman Smolski won the first trick with the ♢A switching to the ♡J. After cashing three hearts tricks Tony Forrester switched to the ♣6. Declarer took East's ♣J with the ace, played the ♠3 to the king, and the ♠5 back to the queen which was allowed to hold the trick. When declarer then led the ♠5 Forrester ruffed with the ♠10, cashed the ♠A to continue with the ♢8, and this cost dummy's last trump. Declarer had to lose another diamond and a club—and went three down.

Solution Number 45

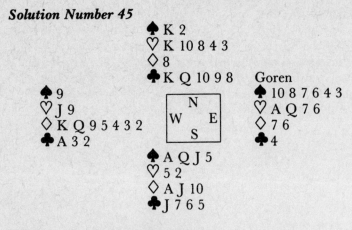

```
            ♠ K 2
            ♡ K 10 8 4 3
            ◇ 8
            ♣ K Q 10 9 8      Goren
♠ 9                    ┌─────────┐   ♠ 10 8 7 6 4 3
♡ J 9                  │    N    │   ♡ A Q 7 6
◇ K Q 9 5 4 3 2        │ W     E │   ◇ 7 6
♣ A 3 2                │    S    │   ♣ 4
                       └─────────┘
            ♠ A Q J 5
            ♡ 5 2
            ◇ A J 10
            ♣ J 7 6 5
```

Duplicate in USA, about 1950.

Contract: 3 No Trumps redoubled. Lead ♡J.

That the opening lead was lucky is beyond any doubt. It was perfectly normal that Charles Goren should take dummy's ♡K with the ace and then switch to the ◇7, but the point may be seen later. Declarer covered with the ◇10, West won with the ◇Q and played the ♡9. Now declarer ducked with the ♡3 from dummy, but nevertheless Goren went up with the ♡Q—so establishing three heart tricks for declarer—to be able to get in and lead the ◇6. Thus West's diamonds were set up while he still held the ♣A as an entry and a stopper. Declarer could not make more than eight tricks.

The same defence was found many years ago by Mrs C. E. Travers in a duplicate in USA—but that was in a trump contract.

Deal Number 46

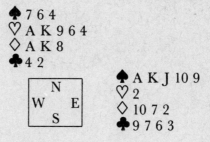

♠ 7 6 4
♡ A K 9 6 4
◇ A K 8
♣ 4 2

♠ A K J 10 9
♡ 2
◇ 10 7 2
♣ 9 7 6 3

North/East–West.
The bidding:

North	South
1 ♡	2 NT
3 NT	

West leads the ♠3. How does East plan the defence?

Deal Number 47

♠ 7 6 4
♡ A Q J 10
◇ J 9 8 3
♣ 8 3

♠ K
♡ 9 7 6 5 3 2
◇ 7 4
♣ K J 6 2

♠
♡
◇
♣

West/None.
The bidding:

West	North	East	South
Pass	Pass	1 ◇	4 ♠

West leads the ◇7. East wins the ◇Q and K and continues with the ◇6. South ruffs with the ♠J. How should West plan his defence?

Deal Number 48

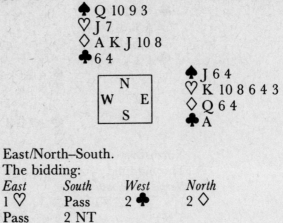

♠ Q 10 9 3
♡ J 7
◇ A K J 10 8
♣ 6 4

♠ J 6 4
♡ K 10 8 6 4 3
◇ Q 6 4
♣ A

East/North–South.
The bidding:

East	South	West	North
1 ♡	Pass	2 ♣	2 ◇
Pass	2 NT		

West leads the ♣10. East wins and switches to the ♠6. Declarer wins the trick with the ♣7, plays the ◇9, ducking with the ◇8 in dummy. How does East continue the defence?

Solution Number 46

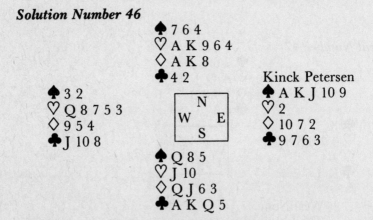

♠ 7 6 4
♡ A K 9 6 4
◇ A K 8
♣ 4 2

Kinck Petersen
♠ A K J 10 9
♡ 2
◇ 10 7 2
♣ 9 7 6 3

♠ 3 2
♡ Q 8 7 5 3
◇ 9 5 4
♣ J 10 8

♠ Q 8 5
♡ J 10
◇ Q J 6 3
♣ A K Q 5

Duplicate in Copenhagen, January 1965.
Contract: 3 No Trumps. Lead ♠3.
Mrs Gerda Kinck Petersen could hardly believe her eyes when she saw such a dream lead as a low spade, but she was fully aware that her partner had tried to find what could be declarer's weakness. She won with the ♠K and continued with

72

the ♠J. In the possible hope of some sort of blocking, declarer ducked but Mrs Kinck Petersen took the remaining spades, and so the contract went one down.

South was the first to congratulate his opponent on her clever defence unaware that Robert Jordan had done the same in a World Champion match against Argentina in 1963 at St Vincent.

Solution Number 47

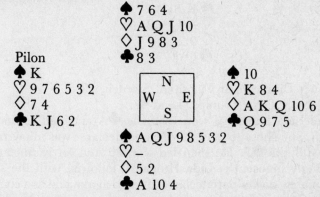

```
                    ♠ 7 6 4
                    ♡ A Q J 10
                    ◇ J 9 8 3
                    ♣ 8 3
Pilon
♠ K                           ♠ 10
♡ 9 7 6 5 3 2    N            ♡ K 8 4
◇ 7 4          W   E          ◇ A K Q 10 6
♣ K J 6 2         S           ♣ Q 9 7 5
                    ♠ A Q J 9 8 5 3 2
                    ♡ –
                    ◇ 5 2
                    ♣ A 10 4
```

French Trials for the European Championships at Elsinore, 1978.

Contract: 4♠. Lead ◇7.

East played the ◇Q and K and continued with the ◇6. Declarer ruffed with the ♠J. At the other table West overruffed with the ♠K switching to clubs. But as a result declarer could use two of dummy's trumps as entries and set up hearts for the discard of his losing clubs. However, Dominique Pilon did not overruff, and dropped instead a club, taking the risk of course that declarer would draw the ♠A. But why should he have done that?

He was certain in his own mind that East held the ♠K and, thus having no trump losers he decided to lose a club, ruff another club, discard the last club on the ♡A, and then finesse the ♠K. All went well until the trump finesse when Pilon suddenly came up with the ♠K and the cold contract went one down.

I think that I should add here that this defence won the prize for the world's best hand of the year.

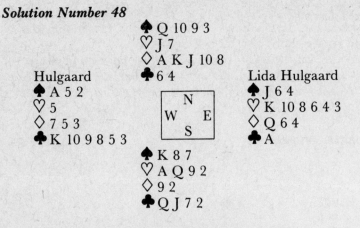

♠ Q 10 9 3
♡ J 7
♢ A K J 10 8
♣ 6 4

Hulgaard
♠ A 5 2
♡ 5
♢ 7 5 3
♣ K 10 9 8 5 3

Lida Hulgaard
♠ J 6 4
♡ K 10 8 6 4 3
♢ Q 6 4
♣ A

♠ K 8 7
♡ A Q 9 2
♢ 9 2
♣ Q J 7 2

Summer Duplicate at Tylosand, Sweden, 1963.

Contract: 2 No Trumps. Lead ♣10.

Mrs Lida Hulgaard won with the ♣A and had to find a switch. She chose to play the ♠6 and declarer was allowed to win with the ♠7. He then led the ♢9 and let it run and, seemingly innocently, Lida Hulgaard followed with the ♢6. Fortunately on her part declarer finessed again, and as a consequence the defenders' efforts were directed on blocking dummy. Winning with the ♢Q Lida Hulgaard then played the ♠J, and so declarer was allowed to win with the ♠K. A third spade Johs Hulgaard had to win, and he switched to the ♣9. Declarer won. He then tried a low heart to dummy's jack. Lida Hulgaard won with the king and had to continue in hearts. Declarer finessed with the ♡9, but the end result was that he had to lose two clubs to West, and went one down.

It is clear that it had not helped to play the ♠8 to the fifth trick, for then Johs Hulgaard would have won with the ♠A and put declarer in again on the king.

Deal Number 49

                        ♠ A 7
                        ♡ A J 9 5 2
                        ◇ 9 6 4 3
                        ♣ Q 10

♠ K J
♡ 6 3
◇ Q J 10 8
♣ 9 7 6 5 2

South/North–South.
The bidding:

South	North
2 NT	3 ♡
3 NT	5 NT
6 NT	

West leads the ◇Q which is allowed to hold the trick. How does West continue?

Deal Number 50

                        ♠ 10 4 2
                        ♡ K 4
                        ◇ J 9 7 3
                        ♣ Q 6 5 3

♠ K 9 8 6 5
♡ A J   N
◇ K 10 5 2   W   E
♣ K 4   S

West/Both.
The bidding:

West	North	East	South
1 ♠	Pass	Pass	1 NT
Pass	2 NT	Pass	3 NT

West leads the ♠6 and East follows with the ♠3. Declarer wins with the ♣Q, lays down the ♣A and continues with the ♣9. How does West continue the defence?

Deal Number 51

♠ 10 9 7 2
♡ A K 8
◇ 10 8 7
♣ K 5 3

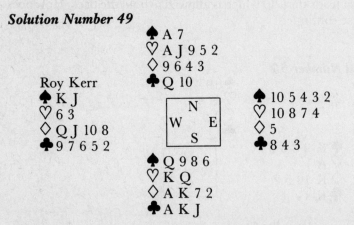

North/East–West.
The bidding:

North	South
Pass	2 ♣
2 ♡	3 ◇
3 ♠	4 ♣
4 ♡	4 NT
5 ♣	6 ◇

What does West lead?

Solution Number 49

♠ A 7
♡ A J 9 5 2
◇ 9 6 4 3
♣ Q 10

Roy Kerr
♠ K J
♡ 6 3
◇ Q J 10 8
♣ 9 7 6 5 2

♠ 10 5 4 3 2
♡ 10 8 7 4
◇ 5
♣ 8 4 3

♠ Q 9 8 6
♡ K Q
◇ A K 7 2
♣ A K J

World Championships in Venice, 1974. France-New Zealand.
Contract: 6 No Trumps. Lead ◇Q.

Roy Kerr led the ◇Q and was allowed to hold the trick. He could see that declarer probably had ten tricks without the spades and that he was himself in great danger of a squeeze if declarer had the ♣Q in the closed hand. But to carry out a squeeze it was necessary for declarer to keep the ♠A in dummy.

76

Roy Kerr decided, therefore, to take the bull by the horns and led the ♠J! Declarer was not inclined to risk going down at once for there might still be a chance of three diamond tricks, so he went up with dummy's ace—and went down one.

Solution Number 50

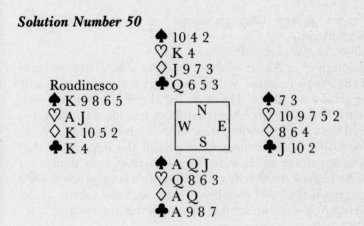

```
              ♠ 10 4 2
              ♡ K 4
              ◇ J 9 7 3
              ♣ Q 6 5 3
Roudinesco
♠ K 9 8 6 5               ♠ 7 3
♡ A J          N          ♡ 10 9 7 5 2
◇ K 10 5 2   W   E        ◇ 8 6 4
♣ K 4          S          ♣ J 10 2
              ♠ A Q J
              ♡ Q 8 6 3
              ◇ A Q
              ♣ A 9 8 7
```

European Championships in Dublin, 1967. France-Greece.
Contract: 3 No Trumps. Lead ♣6.

Declarer won with the ♣Q, laid down the ♣A and continued with the ♣9. But on the ♣A Jean-Marc Roudinesco had unblocked the king, so East took the third club trick and could continue spades from the right side while West still stopped both the red suits. Two down.

A similar unblocking play with almost the same purpose was carried out by:
Clifford W. Bishop in a University Duplicate in Chicago, 1961.
Dennis Sullivan in Los Angeles, 1966.
Meyer Schleifer in USA, 1967.

Solution Number 51

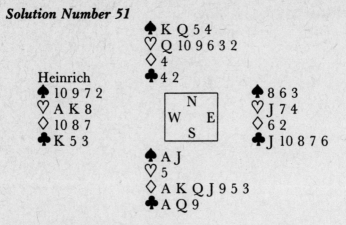

♠ K Q 5 4
♡ Q 10 9 6 3 2
◇ 4
♣ 4 2

Heinrich
♠ 10 9 7 2
♡ A K 8
◇ 10 8 7
♣ K 5 3

♠ 8 6 3
♡ J 7 4
◇ 6 2
♣ J 10 8 7 6

♠ A J
♡ 5
◇ A K Q J 9 5 3
♣ A Q 9

European Junior Championships in Copenhagen, 1974.
Israel-Austria.

Contract: 6◇. Lead ♣10.

Heinrich from Austria did not lead the ♡K. If declarer was told that West held the ♡A-K the stage was set for a deadly squeeze. To avoid this Heinrich led the ♣10. Declarer won with the ♣A and ran seven rounds of trumps. Heinrich discarded first two low clubs, then the ♡8 and the ♡K.

From this declarer must have gained the impression that West's remaining cards were three spades and the doubleton ♣K. So he took the ♠J over with dummy's king, threw the ♣9 on dummy's ♠Q and endplayed West with the fourth spade. But Heinrich took the setting trick with the 'impossible' ♡A.

Deal Number 52

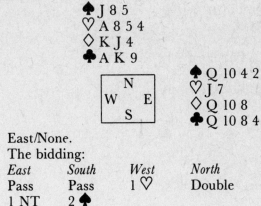

♠ J 8 5
♡ A 8 5 4
◇ K J 4
♣ A K 9

♠ Q 10 4 2
♡ J 7
◇ Q 10 8
♣ Q 10 8 4

East/None.
The bidding:

East	South	West	North
Pass	Pass	1 ♡	Double
1 NT	2 ♠		

West leads the ♡K. Declarer wins with dummy's ace, draws one round of trumps with the ♠5 to the king in the closed hand and continues with three rounds of clubs from the top. How does East plan the defence?

Deal Number 53

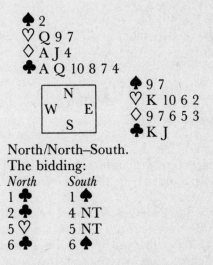

♠ 2
♡ Q 9 7
◇ A J 4
♣ A Q 10 8 7 4

♠ 9 7
♡ K 10 6 2
◇ 9 7 6 5 3
♣ K J

North/North–South.
The bidding:

North	South
1 ♣	1 ♠
2 ♣	4 NT
5 ♡	5 NT
6 ♣	6 ♠

West leads the ♣6. Declarer wins with the ♠J and draws the three highest spades, West following. Then declarer leads a low club to dummy's queen. How does East plan the defence?

Deal Number 54

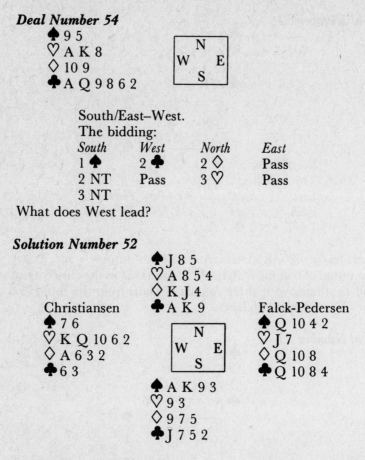

♠ 9 5
♡ A K 8
◇ 10 9
♣ A Q 9 8 6 2

South/East–West.
The bidding:

South	West	North	East
1 ♠	2 ♣	2 ◇	Pass
2 NT	Pass	3 ♡	Pass
3 NT			

What does West lead?

Solution Number 52

♠ J 8 5
♡ A 8 5 4
◇ K J 4
♣ A K 9

Christiansen
♠ 7 6
♡ K Q 10 6 2
◇ A 6 3 2
♣ 6 3

Falck-Pedersen
♠ Q 10 4 2
♡ J 7
◇ Q 10 8
♣ Q 10 8 4

♠ A K 9 3
♡ 9 3
◇ 9 7 5
♣ J 7 5 2

Trials for European Championships in Oslo, Norway, 1950.
Contract: 2♠. Lead ♡K.

Declarer won with dummy's ace, played the ♠5 to the ♠K in the closed hand and switched to three rounds of clubs from the top.

Leif Falck-Pedersen followed with the ♣10 to the third round! He thus kept the control of the suit whilst Leif Christiansen ruffed with a worthless trump—and switched to the ◇2! Falck-Pedersen took dummy's ◇J with the queen and switched to the ♠4. Declarer successfully finessed with the ♠9 and played the ◇7 to dummy's king, when Christiansen discarded first a low heart and then a low diamond.

A low heart from dummy was taken by Falck-Pedersen who played the ♠Q, which declarer took with the ♠A. Christiansen again discarded a low heart in order to be able to keep the connection open to East with a low diamond. He succeeded as declarer now played the ◇9, taken by East with the ◇10. Falck-Pedersen drew declarer's last trump and took the under-trick with the ♣Q.

If West blanks the ◇A and wins it, declarer would get his low trump 'en passant'.

Solution Number 53

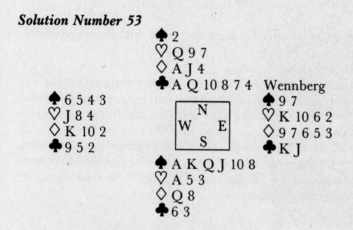

```
                    ♠ 2
                    ♡ Q 9 7
                    ◇ A J 4
                    ♣ A Q 10 8 7 4   Wennberg
   ♠ 6 5 4 3              N          ♠ 9 7
   ♡ J 8 4          W         E      ♡ K 10 6 2
   ◇ K 10 2              S           ◇ 9 7 6 5 3
   ♣ 9 5 2                           ♣ K J
                    ♠ A K Q J 10 8
                    ♡ A 5 3
                    ◇ Q 8
                    ♣ 6 3
```

Duplicate in Stockholm, Sweden, in the 40's.

Contract: 6♠. Lead ♣6.

After four rounds of trumps declarer played the ♣6 to dummy's ♣Q. Seth Wennberg had already seen that a bold move was necessary as West had not found the killing lead of a heart, and so he followed with—the ♣J.

No one could blame declarer for placing West with four clubs to the king. He calculated taking the rest with another club finesse, then setting up the suit with a ruff, and with the ◇A as an entry to the good clubs. But to re-enter the closed hand he had to use the ♡A. He then played the ♣3 to dummy's ♣10. It was at that point Wennberg won with the ♣K and cashed the ♡K, which declarer himself had set up for him.

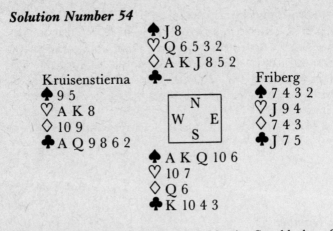

♠ J 8
♡ Q 6 5 3 2
◊ A K J 8 5 2
♣ —

Kruisenstierna
♠ 9 5
♡ A K 8
◊ 10 9
♣ A Q 9 8 6 2

Friberg
♠ 7 4 3 2
♡ J 9 4
◊ 7 4 3
♣ J 7 5

♠ A K Q 10 6
♡ 10 7
◊ Q 6
♣ K 10 4 3

Mixed-Pairs World Championship in Stockholm, Sweden, 1970.

Contract: 3 No Trumps.

In sheer desperation Douglas von Kruisenstierna led the ♡8! If the Finnish lady sitting South had had the nerve to go up with dummy's ♡Q she would have scored a clean top with twelve tricks as most of the pairs played 4 ♠, making five.

But declarer let it run to the closed hand so that it was Elna Friberg who won the trick with the ♡J. She switched at once to clubs, and with two clubs and three hearts to East–West the contract went down one.

Deal Number 55

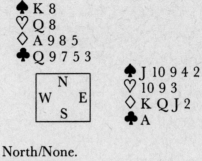

♠ K 8
♡ Q 8
◇ A 9 8 5
♣ Q 9 7 5 3

♠ J 10 9 4 2
♡ 10 9 3
◇ K Q J 2
♣ A

North/None.
The bidding:

North	South
Pass	1♠
2♣	2♡
2 NT	4♡

West leads the ◇7. Declarer wins with dummy's ace and plays the ♣3 which East must win. What does East lead now?

Deal Number 56

♠ 9 6 5 3 2
♡ J 8
◇ A 9 6 2
♣ J 2

♠ A
♡ A 10 6
◇ K J 7 5 4
♣ Q 10 8 5

South/Both.
The bidding:

South	West	North	East
1◇	Double	2◇	Pass
Pass	Double		

West leads the ♠4. How does East plan the defence?

Deal Number 57

```
              ♠ 6
              ♡ J 8 7 5 3
              ◇ Q J 6
              ♣ K J 10 9
♠ A 9 7 2                      N
♡ K Q 4                    W       E
◇ 9 7 3                        S
♣ 8 6 4
```

South/None.
The bidding:

South	West	North	East
1 ◇	Pass	1 ♡	1 ♠
2 NT	Pass	3 NT	Pass
Pass	Double	ReDouble	

West leads the ♣2. East wins with the ♣K and returns the ♣5. South covers with the ♣10. How does West continue the defence?

Solution Number 55

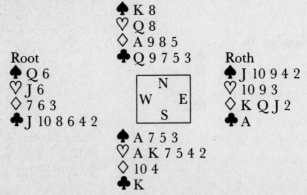

```
                  ♠ K 8
                  ♡ Q 8
                  ◇ A 9 8 5
Root              ♣ Q 9 7 5 3       Roth
♠ Q 6                               ♠ J 10 9 4 2
♡ J 6                 N             ♡ 10 9 3
◇ 7 6 3           W       E         ◇ K Q J 2
♣ J 10 8 6 4 2        S             ♣ A
                  ♠ A 7 5 3
                  ♡ A K 7 5 4 2
                  ◇ 10 4
                  ♣ K
```

World Championships, Miami, 1967. Round-robin Italy-USA.

Contract: 4♡. Lead ◇7.

It was declarer's plan to ruff a spade, but he had first to set up the ♣Q on which to discard the fourth spade. So he went up with dummy's ◇A to then play the ♣3, which East had to win. Many players would almost certainly now have tried to cash some diamond tricks, but Alvin Roth switched immediately to the ♡9 which was taken by dummy's queen. When declarer tried to cash the ♣Q Roth ruffed with the ♡3 and was over-ruffed. Declarer then played three rounds of spades, but thanks to Roth's earlier lead of the ♡9 William Root could ruff with the ♡J and set Roth in in diamonds, with the consequence that Roth could remove dummy's last trump with the ♡10 and secure the undertrick in spades.

Solution Number 56

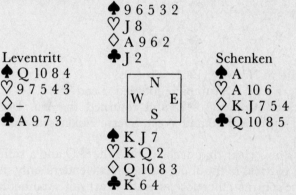

♠ 9 6 5 3 2
♡ J 8
◇ A 9 6 2
♣ J 2

Leventritt
♠ Q 10 8 4
♡ 9 7 5 4 3
◇ –
♣ A 9 7 3

Schenken
♠ A
♡ A 10 6
◇ K J 7 5 4
♣ Q 10 8 5

♠ K J 7
♡ K Q 2
◇ Q 10 8 3
♣ K 6 4

Teams-of-four Match in USA, 1967.
Contract: 2◇ doubled. Lead ♠4.

Peter Leventritt's double was based upon his distribution and even then made on too small values, and he bitterly regretted what he had done when Howard Schenken changed it into a penalty double.

Winning with the ♠A Schenken immediately switched to a low trump. Declarer won with the ◇8 and played the ♡2 to dummy's jack. Schenken won with the ♡A, to continue with another low trump. Declarer won with the ◇10 and cashed two high hearts in order to discard a club from dummy, then he led the ♣4 to dummy's jack. Schenken won with the ♣Q and for the third time led a trump. Declarer won with the ◇Q and laid down the ♣K, but Schenken ruffed and led a fourth round of trumps. Dummy won with the ◇A and had to play spades to Leventritt who had thrown all his clubs and now took the rest—down two!

```
                    ♠ 6
                    ♡ J 8 7 5 3
                    ◇ Q J 6
    Mikkelsen       ♣ K J 10 9
    ♠ A 9 7 2                          ♠ K J 8 5 3
    ♡ K Q 4         ┌─────────┐        ♡ A 9
    ◇ 9 7 3         │    N    │        ◇ 8 4 2
    ♣ 8 6 4         │ W     E │        ♣ 7 5 3
                    │    S    │
                    └─────────┘
                    ♠ Q 10 4
                    ♡ 10 6 2
                    ◇ A K 10 5
                    ♣ A Q 2
```

Duplicate in Norway, 1961.

Contract: 3 No Trumps redoubled. Lead ♣2.

East won with the ♣K and returned the ♣5. Declarer covered with the ♣10 and West, Sverre Mikkelsen, won with the ♣A.

It was now clear that declarer held the ♣Q and a sufficient number of tricks in the minor suits. The defenders' only chance to set the contract, therefore, was the heart suit. At other tables where the contract was 3 No Trumps West tried the ♡K to see East's reaction, and then the third heart was blocked.

Mikkelsen believed that the only chance was that East held the ♡A, but at the same time he felt that the ace might be a doubleton. So he led the ♡4! His foresight was rewarded —East-West took three heart tricks, and the redoubled contract went down one.

Deal Number 58

♠ K 6
♡ Q 8 7 2
♢ A J 4 3
♣ Q J 2

```
      N
  W       E
      S
```

South/Both.
The bidding:

South	North
1 ♡	2 ♣
2 ♢	3 ♣
3 NT	

What card does West lead?

Deal Number 59

♠ J 8 7 2
♡ 10 9 8 4
♢ 5 4
♣ J 9 3

♠ 9 6
♡ K 7 6 2
♢ 10 6
♣ Q 10 8 7 4

```
      N
  W       E
      S
```

North/East–West.
The bidding:

North	South
Pass	2 ♣
2 ♢	3 ♢
3 ♡	3 NT

West leads the ♣7 and dummy's ♣9 wins the trick. From dummy the ♢5 is led, declarer finessing with the ♢8. How does West continue the defence?

Deal Number 60

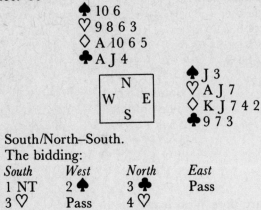

♠ 10 6
♡ 9 8 6 3
◇ A 10 6 5
♣ A J 4

♠ J 3
♡ A J 7
◇ K J 7 4 2
♣ 9 7 3

South/North–South.
The bidding:

South	West	North	East
1 NT	2 ♠	3 ♣	Pass
3 ♡	Pass	4 ♡	

West leads the ◇8 and dummy follows with the ◇5. How does East plan the defence?

Solution Number 58

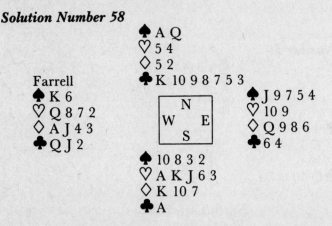

♠ A Q
♡ 5 4
◇ 5 2
♣ K 10 9 8 7 5 3

Farrell
♠ K 6
♡ Q 8 7 2
◇ A J 4 3
♣ Q J 2

♠ J 9 7 5 4
♡ 10 9
◇ Q 9 8 6
♣ 6 4

♠ 10 8 3 2
♡ A K J 6 3
◇ K 10 7
♣ A

Spring Nationals, Ladies' Championships, St Louis, 1973.
Contract: 3 No Trumps.

Hoping to find partner with spades Mary Jane Farrell led the ♠K!

It was a most fortunate lead as it blocked dummy's clubs. After having cashed the blank ♣A declarer now missed one entry to dummy to set up the clubs and to be able to cash them. By cashing the ♠Q and the ♣K, followed by continuously

leading hearts, declarer set up a third heart and thus forced
West to lead diamonds. But even so the contract went down one.

Solution Number 59

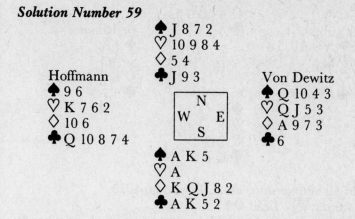

♠ J 8 7 2
♡ 10 9 8 4
◇ 5 4
♣ J 9 3

Hoffmann
♠ 9 6
♡ K 7 6 2
◇ 10 6
♣ Q 10 8 7 4

Von Dewitz
♠ Q 10 4 3
♡ Q J 5 3
◇ A 9 7 3
♣ 6

♠ A K 5
♡ A
◇ K Q J 8 2
♣ A K 5 2

International Congress at Eastbourne, February 1973.
   Contract: 3 No Trumps. Lead ♣7.
   Dummy's ♣9 won the first trick and the ◇5 was led, declarer
finishing with the ◇8. The young British player Martin Hoffman won with the ◇10—and switched to the ♡2! The German
Egmont von Dewitz could count to 13 and ducked, and declarer
won with the blank ace. Declarer had to set up diamonds,
East-West took their three heart tricks—and the contract went
down one.

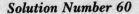

```
                    ♠ 10 6
                    ♡ 9 8 6 3
                    ◇ A 10 6 5
Garozzo             ♣ A J 4         Belladonna
♠ A 9 8 7 5 4                       ♠ J 3
♡ 5 2                               ♡ A J 7
◇ 8                                 ◇ K J 7 4 2
♣ Q 10 8 5                          ♣ 9 7 3
                    ♠ K Q 2
                    ♡ K Q 10 4
                    ◇ Q 9 3
                    ♣ K 6 2
```

World Championship, Final, Bermuda, 1975.

Contract: 4♡. Lead ◇8.

This was the hand which at last, when only ten hands remained to be played, brought Italy into the lead after having trailed for most of the time (after 52 of the 96 deals even with as much as 78 international match points).

The contract and the lead were identical at the two tables, but in the other room declarer went up with the ◇A and played trumps. East, Robert Hamman won with the ♡A, cashed the ◇K and gave Robert Wolff a diamond ruff so that the contract went one down.

Giorgio Belladonna, on the other hand, won the first trick with the ◇K, but he did not play another diamond immediately and instead switched to the ♠J, covered by the ♠Q and taken with the ♠A. Benito Garozzo led another spade to dummy's ♠10. When declarer now played a trump Belladonna went up with the ace, gave Garozzo the delayed diamond ruff, and was himself now able to overruff dummy on a spade from Garozzo, so that the contract went two down.

Deal Number 61

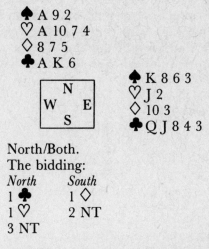

♠ A 9 2
♡ A 10 7 4
◇ 8 7 5
♣ A K 6

♠ K 8 6 3
♡ J 2
◇ 10 3
♣ Q J 8 4 3

North/Both.
The bidding:

North	South
1 ♣	1 ◇
1 ♡	2 NT
3 NT	

West leads the ♠Q, holds the trick and continues with the ♠J which declarer takes with dummy's ace to play a heart to the queen in the closed hand. West wins with the ♡K and continues with the ♠5. East wins with the ♠K and declarer follows with the ♠10. How does East continue?

Deal Number 62

♠ 8 4
♡ 8 5 2
◇ J 10 8
♣ K 10 9 4 3

♠ Q
♡ A K J 10
◇ Q 9 7 4
♣ Q 7 6 2

West/None.
The bidding:

West	North	East	South
1 ♡	Pass	Pass	Double
Pass	2 ♣	Pass	2 NT

West leads the ♡K and switches to the ♣7. Dummy follows with the ♣9, East the ♣5 and declarer wins with the ♣A.

91

Declarer plays the ♢2 to dummy's ♢10, West ducking, and the ♠4 from dummy, East following with the ♠3 and declarer the ♠2. West wins with the ♠Q and continues with the ♠2, dummy winning with the king. Declarer drops the ♠5 and plays the ♠8 to the ace in the closed hand. What card does West discard?

Deal Number 63

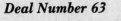

```
                    ♠ K 5 3
                    ♡ –
                    ♢ A Q 9 4 3 2
                    ♣ A Q 7 6
  ♠ A 10 4 2            N
  ♡ Q 8 6 3
  ♢ 7 6              W     E
  ♣ 9 3 2               S
```

North/North–South.
The bidding:

North	East	South	West
1 ♢	2 ♣	2 ♠	Pass
2 NT	Pass	3 ♡	Pass
3 ♠	Pass	4 ♠	

West leads the ♣3. Declarer wins with dummy's ace and plays the ♠3 to the ♠Q in the closed hand. How does West plan the defence?

Solution Number 61

```
                    ♠ A 9 2
                    ♡ A 10 7 4
                    ♢ 8 7 5
                    ♣ A K 6            Rolf Boe
  ♠ Q J 5                              ♠ K 8 6 3
  ♡ K 8 5 3            N               ♡ J 2
  ♢ J 6 4           W     E            ♢ 10 3
  ♣ 10 5 2             S               ♣ Q J 8 4 3
                    ♠ 10 7 4
                    ♡ Q 9 6
                    ♢ A K Q 9 2
                    ♣ 9 7
```

92

Duplicate in Oslo, Norway, 1943.

Contract: 3 No Trumps. Lead ♠Q, then ♠J.

Declarer won the second spade with dummy's ace. He played the ♡4 to the queen which West took with the king to continue with the ♠5. Rolf Boe won with the king, and now what? Did he hurry to cash the thirteenth spade? Boe did nothing of the sort—he switched to the ♣J and made declarer believe that West held the ♠8.

Declarer won with dummy's ♣K and ran five diamonds. In dummy he kept the ♡A-10 and the ♣A. West kept two hearts and one club and East the ♠8, the ♡J and the ♣Q.

It was a duplicate where an overtrick would be worth its weight in gold. Since West was 'marked' with the last spade, declarer thought that there could be no risk in trying to make four by a finesse with the ♡10. But Rolf Boe won with the blank jack and then cashed the ♠8 with the result that the contract was down one, declarer being lucky enough to retain the right ace in dummy.

Solution Number 62

```
                    ♠ 8 4
                    ♡ 8 5 2
                    ◇ J 10 8
                    ♣ K 10 9 4 3
   Slavenburg                        Kreijns
   ♠ Q              ┌─────────┐      ♠ K J 10 7 3
   ♡ A K J 10       │    N    │      ♡ 9 6 4
   ◇ Q 9 7 4        │ W     E │      ◇ 6 3
   ♣ Q 7 6 2        │    S    │      ♣ J 8 5
                    └─────────┘
                    ♠ A 9 6 5 2
                    ♡ Q 7 3
                    ◇ A K 5 2
                    ♣ A
```

European Championships, Ostende, 1965. Holland-Great Britain.

Contract: 2 No Trumps. Lead ♡K.

Cornelius Slavenburg switched to the ♣7. Hans Kreijns ducked dummy's ♣9 with the ♣5, and declarer won with the ♣A. He played the ◇2 and as Slavenburg ducked, dummy's ◇10 won the trick and the ♠4 was led. East and South ducked and Slavenburg won with the ♠Q to continue with the ♠2 to

93

dummy's king, declarer dropping the ♠5. Then he led the ♠8, took East's ♠10 with the ace and played the ♡Q, intending to endplay West hoping he would have to lead from the ♢Q after having cashed his hearts.

But on the ♠A Slavenburg had jettisoned the ♣Q! Having cashed his three hearts he could play the ♣6 to Kreijns who took the rest in spades—and the contract was down four.

Solution Number 63

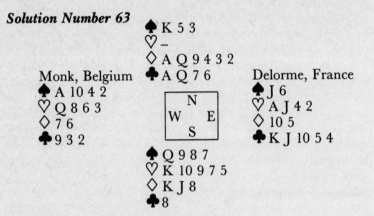

```
                    ♠ K 5 3
                    ♡ –
                    ♢ A Q 9 4 3 2
Monk, Belgium       ♣ A Q 7 6        Delorme, France
♠ A 10 4 2                           ♠ J 6
♡ Q 8 6 3              N             ♡ A J 4 2
♢ 7 6             W       E          ♢ 10 5
♣ 9 3 2               S             ♣ K J 10 5 4
                    ♠ Q 9 8 7
                    ♡ K 10 9 7 5
                    ♢ K J 8
                    ♣ 8
```

Duplicate at Enghien, France, 1970.
Contract: 4♠. Lead ♣3.

Declarer won with dummy's ace and led the ♠3 to the queen. Monk coolly ducked with the ♠2. Declarer now believed East to hold the ♠A. He played the ♠9 and therefore let it run when Charles Monk ducked again with the ♠4. Jacques Delorme, winning with the blank ♠J, switched to the ♡2. Declarer covered with the ♡10 and ruffed Monk's ♡Q with dummy's ♠K. Hoping that the two outstanding trumps would fall together he played a diamond to the king and laid down the ♠8, but Monk won and drew declarer's last trump. He then played ♣9 and continued with the ♣2 to Delorme's three club tricks, so the contract was down five.

As a comment here my long-held maxim 'Never lead the top of nothing but the next highest unless they be equals' is clearly demonstrated, for if Monk had not saved the ♣9 declarer might well have won two more tricks.

Deal Number 64

♠ J 9 7
♡ Q 8 6 2
♢ 7 6 5 2
♣ 8 2

♠ 8
♡ K 9 5 4
♢ A 10 9 4 3
♣ K Q 3

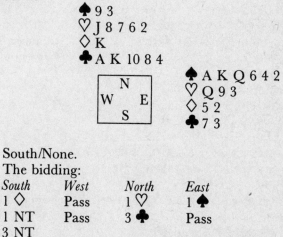

North/East–West.
The bidding:

North	East	South	West
Pass	Pass	1 ♠	Pass
Pass	1 NT	2 ♣	2 ♢
2 ♠			

West leads the ♣8. East covers dummy's ♣9 with the 10 and declarer wins with the ♣K. Declarer leads the ♣10. How does West plan the defence?

Deal Number 65

♠ 9 3
♡ J 8 7 6 2
♢ K
♣ A K 10 8 4

♠ A K Q 6 4 2
♡ Q 9 3
♢ 5 2
♣ 7 3

South/None.
The bidding:

South	West	North	East
1 ♢	Pass	1 ♡	1 ♠
1 NT	Pass	3 ♣	Pass
3 NT			

West leads the ♠7. How should East plan the defence?

Deal Number 66

       ♠ 7 4
       ♡ A 8 6 4 2
       ◇ J 3
       ♣ K Q 8 4

♠ A K J 9 5
♡ K 10 9
◇ A 10 6
♣ 9 6

```
   N
W     E
   S
```

North/None.
The bidding:

North	East	South	West
Pass	Pass	1 ◇	Double
ReDouble	Pass	Pass	1 ♠
2 ♡	Pass	2 NT	

West draws the ♠K. What does West play next—after having seen dummy's cards?

Solution Number 64

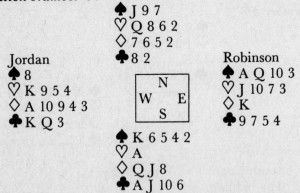

       ♠ J 9 7
       ♡ Q 8 6 2
       ◇ 7 6 5 2
       ♣ 8 2

Jordan   Robinson
♠ 8   ♠ A Q 10 3
♡ K 9 5 4   ♡ J 10 7 3
◇ A 10 9 4 3   ◇ K
♣ K Q 3   ♣ 9 7 5 4

```
   N
W     E
   S
```

       ♠ K 6 5 4 2
       ♡ A
       ◇ Q J 8
       ♣ A J 10 6

Bridge Olympiad, New York, 1964, 11th round, USA–South Africa.

Contract: 2♠. Lead ♣8.

Arthur Robinson covered dummy's ♠9 with the ♠10. Declarer won with the ♠K and played the ♣10. Robert Jordan

won with the ♣Q and switched to the ◇3. Robinson got on lead
with the ◇K so that he could draw two rounds of trumps before
leading the ♣5. Declarer incautiously finessed with the
♣J—and as a result it cost him two tricks. Jordan won with the
♣K, cashed the ◇A and continued with a diamond for Robinson to ruff with the ♣3. He exited in hearts and declarer had to
lose a third club trick—down three.

Solution Number 65

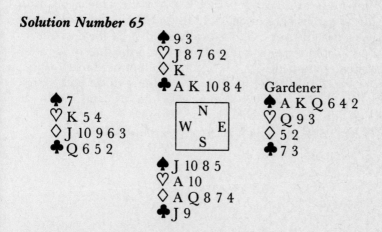

```
              ♠ 9 3
              ♡ J 8 7 6 2
              ◇ K
              ♣ A K 10 8 4         Gardener
  ♠ 7                              ♠ A K Q 6 4 2
  ♡ K 5 4             N            ♡ Q 9 3
  ◇ J 10 9 6 3    W       E        ◇ 5 2
  ♣ Q 6 5 2           S            ♣ 7 3
              ♠ J 10 8 5
              ♡ A 10
              ◇ A Q 8 7 4
              ♣ J 9
```

The Indian Open Championships, to which was invited a
British team. New Delhi, November 1978.
  Contract: 3 No Trumps. Lead ♣7.
  Nicola Gardener cashed two high spades and then switched
to the ♡3. Declarer ducked, West won the trick with the ♡K
and played another heart to remove declarer's entry to the
diamonds. With a lucky club finesse declarer could take five
club tricks but as he could only come to eight tricks by taking
the ◇K over with the ace he went one down.

Solution Number 66

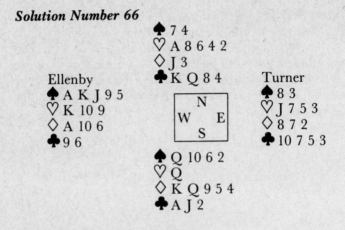

```
              ♠ 7 4
              ♡ A 8 6 4 2
              ◇ J 3
Ellenby       ♣ K Q 8 4       Turner
♠ A K J 9 5       N           ♠ 8 3
♡ K 10 9    W         E       ♡ J 7 5 3
◇ A 10 6          S           ◇ 8 7 2
♣ 9 6                         ♣ 10 7 5 3
              ♠ Q 10 6 2
              ♡ Q
              ◇ K Q 9 5 4
              ♣ A J 2
```

Mixed-Teams in USA, 1968.

Contract: 2 No Trumps. Lead ♠K.

It is quite clear that declarer could stop the spades, and in an effort to get his partner on lead Milton Ellenby switched to the ♡K. Now, this was a fantastically good shift, for declarer let Ellenby hold the king and he had to drop the queen. Astutely Ellenby continued with the ♡10, and dummy ducked again, but now Gloria Turner took the ♡10 over with the jack so that she could shift back to spades, with the just and inevitable result that the contract went one down.

Ellenby's heart switch was the Deschapellos Coup.

Deal Number 67

♠ K 4 2
♡ A 5
♢ K Q J 8 5
♣ 9 6 2

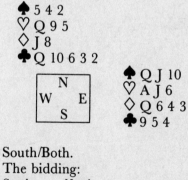

♠ J 9 8 6
♡ 10 6 4
♢ 10 9 7
♣ A K 4

East/Both.
The bidding:

East	South	West	North
1 ♣	Double	Pass	2 ♢
Pass	2 ♡	Pass	3 ♢
Pass	3 NT		

West leads the ♣3. How should East plan the defence?

Deal Number 68

♠ 5 4 2
♡ Q 9 5
♢ J 8
♣ Q 10 6 3 2

♠ Q J 10
♡ A J 6
♢ Q 6 4 3
♣ 9 5 4

South/Both.
The bidding:

South	North
1 ♣	2 ♣
2 NT	

West leads the ♢2. Declarer plays the ♢8 from dummy. How should East plan the defence?

99

Deal Number 69

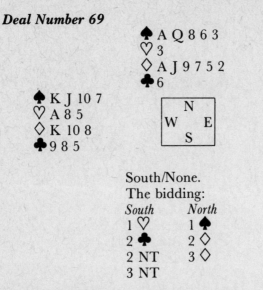

♠ A Q 8 6 3
♡ 3
◇ A J 9 7 5 2
♣ 6

♠ K J 10 7
♡ A 8 5
◇ K 10 8
♣ 9 8 5

South/None.
The bidding:

South	North
1 ♡	1 ♠
2 ♣	2 ◇
2 NT	3 ◇
3 NT	

West leads the ♠J which is taken with the queen in dummy and the ♡3 is played to the queen in the closed hand. West wins with the ace and continues with the ♠K. Dummy wins with the ace and now plays the ◇2 to the queen in the closed hand. How should West plan the defence from here?

Solution Number 67

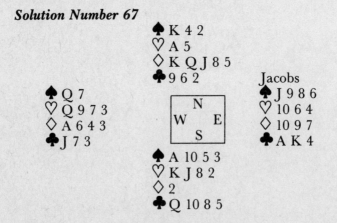

♠ K 4 2
♡ A 5
◇ K Q J 8 5
♣ 9 6 2

Jacobs
♠ J 9 8 6
♡ 10 6 4
◇ 10 9 7
♣ A K 4

♠ Q 7
♡ Q 9 7 3
◇ A 6 4 3
♣ J 7 3

♠ A 10 5 3
♡ K J 8 2
◇ 2
♣ Q 10 8 5

Duplicate in Copenhagen, in the fifties.
Contract: 3 No Trumps. Lead ♣3.

Bo Jacobs went up with the ♣A and returned the ♣4! Declarer finessed with the ♣10. West won with the ♣J and continued with the ♣7 to East's king, but since it was declarer who held the long club Jacobs switched to the ♠9, covered with the ♠10, Q and K. Declarer cashed dummy's ◇K and Q, to which Jacobs followed with the ◇7 and 10(!), and West with the ◇3 and 4. Believing that East now held the blank ace declarer played dummy's ◇5, and Jacobs won with the ◇9. Again he switched, this time to the ♡10, covered with the ♡J, Q and A.

As a consequence declarer could only make seven tricks in all, one in clubs and two in each of the other suits, and went down two.

Solution Number 68

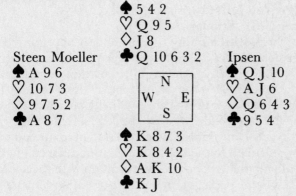

```
                    ♠ 5 4 2
                    ♡ Q 9 5
                    ◇ J 8
  Steen Moeller     ♣ Q 10 6 3 2    Ipsen
  ♠ A 9 6                           ♠ Q J 10
  ♡ 10 7 3            ┌─────┐       ♡ A J 6
  ◇ 9 7 5 2         W │  N  │ E     ◇ Q 6 4 3
  ♣ A 8 7             │  S  │       ♣ 9 5 4
                      └─────┘
                    ♠ K 8 7 3
                    ♡ K 8 4 2
                    ◇ A K 10
                    ♣ K J
```

Danish Open Pairs Championships, Copenhagen, April 1965.
Contract: 2 No Trumps. Lead ◇2.

So as not to give declarer an entry to dummy with the ◇J Thor Ipsen confined himself to a come-on with the ◇6. Declarer won with the ◇10, cashed the ♣K and followed with the ♣J. As Ipsen showed three clubs by first discarding the ♣4, Steffen Steen Moeller won the second round and switched back to diamonds. Declarer tried to reach dummy on the ♡Q, but Ipsen took it with the ace.

In order to protect his partner against an endplay Ipsen then led the ♠Q and took good care that East-West won two of the spade tricks before he switched back to diamonds, and the contract went down one.

Solution Number 69

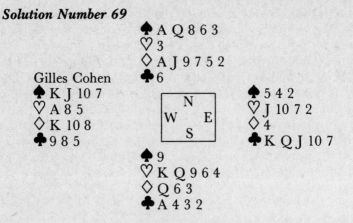

Gilles Cohen

North: ♠ A Q 8 6 3 ♡ 3 ◊ A J 9 7 5 2 ♣ 6

West (Gilles Cohen): ♠ K J 10 7 ♡ A 8 5 ◊ K 10 8 ♣ 9 8 5

East: ♠ 5 4 2 ♡ J 10 7 2 ◊ 4 ♣ K Q J 10 7

South: ♠ 9 ♡ K Q 9 6 4 ◊ Q 6 3 ♣ A 4 3 2

Pairs' Olympiad at New Orleans, 1978.

Contract: 3 No Trumps. Lead ♠J.

Declarer won with dummy's queen and at once played the ♡3 to the queen. Gilles Cohen from France won with the ace, to continue with the ♠K which was taken by dummy's ace, and declarer now did what he should have done in the first place—he led the ◊2 to the queen for Gilles Cohen to duck with the ◊8! When he followed with the ◊10 to the next trick declarer never dreamed that Cohen had sold his diamond trick, being more inclined to the belief that East had risked ducking with the king doubleton. So declarer went up with the ace, and five nice diamond tricks, or six in the present circumstances, were reduced to two.

Here I should add the footnote that this defence won the prize for the best hand at the Olympiad.

Deal Number 70

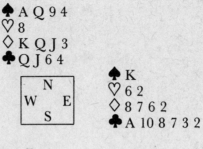

♠ A Q 9 4
♡ 8
◇ K Q J 3
♣ Q J 6 4

                        ♠ K
                        ♡ 6 2
                        ◇ 8 7 6 2
                        ♣ A 10 8 7 3 2

North/Both.
The bidding:

North	South
1 ◇	1 ♠
3 ♠	4 ♠

West leads the ♣9. From dummy comes the ♣4. How does East plan the defence?

Deal Number 71

♠ A 9 4 2
♡ 8 4 2
◇ K 9 3
♣ Q 7 3

                        ♠ J 7 6
                        ♡ J 10 9 5
                        ◇ 8 5 4
                        ♣ A J 2

South/East–West.
The bidding:

South	West	North	East
Pass	1 ♡	Pass	2 ♡
2 ♠	4 ♡	4 ♠	Double

West leads the ♣8. Dummy follows with the ♣3. What card does East play and what is East's lead on his first opportunity?

Deal Number 72

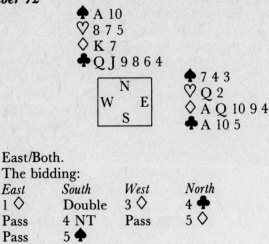

♠ A 10
♡ 8 7 5
◇ K 7
♣ Q J 9 8 6 4

♠ 7 4 3
♡ Q 2
◇ A Q 10 9 4
♣ A 10 5

East/Both.
The bidding:

East	South	West	North
1 ◇	Double	3 ◇	4 ♣
Pass	4 NT	Pass	5 ◇
Pass	5 ♠		

West leads the ◇3, covered by dummy's king. How does East plan the defence?

Solution Number 70

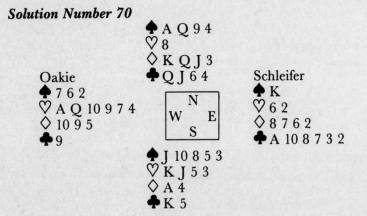

♠ A Q 9 4
♡ 8
◇ K Q J 3
♣ Q J 6 4

Oakie
♠ 7 6 2
♡ A Q 10 9 7 4
◇ 10 9 5
♣ 9

Schleifer
♠ K
♡ 6 2
◇ 8 7 6 2
♣ A 10 8 7 3 2

♠ J 10 8 5 3
♡ K J 5 3
◇ A 4
♣ K 5

Teams-of-four Championship in USA, 1965.
Contract: 4 ♠. Lead ♣9.
East himself was holding so many clubs it seemed highly probable that the lead was a singelton; but if East should have returned a club which was ruffed, then declarer would be in a hurry to draw trumps from the top—which was exactly what

104

happened at the other table. Meyer Schleifer won with the ♣A and then switched to the ♡6. Don Oakie won with the ♡10 and switched to the ◇10. Declarer won with the ◇A, played the ♠J and let it run. Having first got his blank king Schleifer realised that it was opportune to lead a club for Oakie to ruff, with the result that the contract was down one.

Clearly South had never heard of the Rabbi's maxim. It is quite simple if you know and remember it: 'If the king is blank, then play the ace.'

Solution Number 71

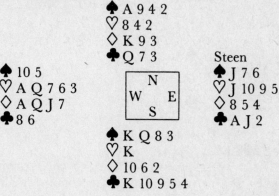

```
                    ♠ A 9 4 2
                    ♡ 8 4 2
                    ◇ K 9 3
                    ♣ Q 7 3
                                      Steen
♠ 10 5                                ♠ J 7 6
♡ A Q 7 6 3         ┌─────────┐       ♡ J 10 9 5
◇ A Q J 7          N│         │        ◇ 8 5 4
♣ 8 6           W  │         │  E     ♣ A J 2
                    │    S    │
                    └─────────┘
                    ♠ K Q 8 3
                    ♡ K
                    ◇ 10 6 2
                    ♣ K 10 9 5 4
```

Duplicate in USA, 1967.

Contract: 4♠ doubled. Lead ♣8.

Douglas Steen let the first club run to declarer's ♣9. After three rounds of trumps declarer played the ♣Q and Steen ducked so as not to give him an entry in the suit. He had to win the next club; it was now essential to set up three tricks before declarer could get discards on the two last clubs. But if a heart was led—and it was quite certain that, at the most, declarer could be holding only one heart—then declarer could reach the closed hand through a heart ruff and then throw two of dummy's diamonds.

Disdaining the guiding principle of leading up to weakness Steen switched to diamonds. The only chance was that West would be strong enough in diamonds, always provided that the suit was led immediately.

West won with the ◇A and played the ◇Q. As was expected

declarer could not get home before West had won one extra trick in each of the red suits, so—one down. Moreover, the ◇A-Q-10 would have been quite enough if the ◇K had been allowed the first trick in the suit.

Solution Number 72

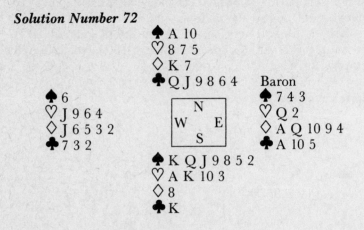

♠ A 10
♡ 8 7 5
◇ K 7
♣ Q J 9 8 6 4

Baron

♠ 6
♡ J 9 6 4
◇ J 6 5 3 2
♣ 7 3 2

♠ 7 4 3
♡ Q 2
◇ A Q 10 9 4
♣ A 10 5

♠ K Q J 9 8 5 2
♡ A K 10 3
◇ 8
♣ K

Duplicate in USA, 1966.
  Contract: 5♠. Lead ◇3.
  Arthur Baron took dummy's ◇K with the ace. It could be accepted as a virtual certainty that declarer could be holding no more diamonds, but there was the possibility that he held some losers in hearts. So Baron switched to the ♠3! Declarer won with dummy's ♠10 and played the ♣4. Baron ducked and let the blank king win. To make that kind of a gift was well worthwhile for otherwise declarer would have got two discards on dummy's clubs. At this point in the game declarer tried to have a heart ruffed by playing three hearts from the top. The third heart went to West's ♡9, but by then Baron had sized up the position and trumped his partner's trick so that he could play another trump. The result was that declarer had to lose a heart trick to West's jack, and went down one.
  A remarkable instance of splendid defence in no less than three different phases of the same deal.

106

Deal Number 73

♠ K 8 4
♡ A 10 9 5
◇ A K Q J 6
♣ J

♠ Q 10 7 5
♡ K 7
◇ 10 8 2
♣ 8 7 5 3

```
      N
  W       E
      S
```

South/Both.
The bidding: (precision)

South	North
Pass	1 ♣
1 ♠	2 ♠
3 ◇	4 ♣
4 ◇	4 ♠
4 NT	5 ♡
5 ♠	

West leads the ♣8. East wins with the ace and switches to the ♡8. Declarer covers with the queen. Does West cover or not?

Deal Number 74

♠ 10 6 3
♡ A 10 9 6
◇ Q 7 5
♣ A 8 6

```
      N
  W       E
      S
```

South/Both.
The bidding:

South	North
1 ♠	1 NT
2 ◇	3 ◇

What card does West lead?

♠ K J 9 3
♡ K Q 4
◇ 5 4
♣ 10 9 5 4

♠ 8 6 5
♡ 10 9 8 7 5
◇ A Q 2
♣ 8 3

South/North–South.
The bidding:
South	*North*
1 NT	3 NT

West leads the ♡10. East takes dummy's queen with the ace, continues with the ♡J which is allowed to hold the trick and the ♡2 to dummy's king. Declarer runs the four top clubs. What does West discard on the two last clubs?

Solution Number 73

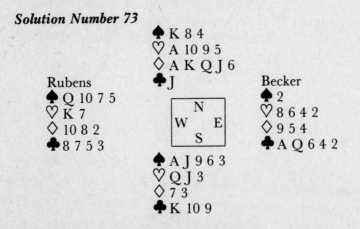

♠ K 8 4
♡ A 10 9 5
◇ A K Q J 6
♣ J

Rubens
♠ Q 10 7 5
♡ K 7
◇ 10 8 2
♣ 8 7 5 3

Becker
♠ 2
♡ 8 6 4 2
◇ 9 5 4
♣ A Q 6 4 2

♠ A J 9 6 3
♡ Q J 3
◇ 7 3
♣ K 10 9

The Vanderbilt Cup at St Louis, Missouri, March 1973.
Contract: 5♠. Lead ♣8.
    B. Jay Becker went up with the ♣A. He then switched to the ♡8, but despite the doubleton Jeff Rubens ducked declarer's ♡Q. Then declarer laid down the ♠A to continue with the ♠3, his intention being to finesse with the ♠8. Rubens effectually

stopped this by playing the ♠10. Dummy won with the king, to continue with the ♠8 to West's queen. It was then that Rubens' foresight was rewarded. He laid down the ♡K, and as he had not covered with the king earlier on declarer could not imagine that it could be a doubleton. The result was that he considered it safest to re-enter the closed hand with the ♡J. Of course Rubens ruffed, and the contract was one down.

Solution Number 74

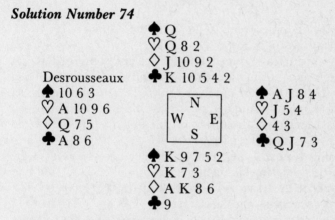

Desrousseaux

Team Championship in France, January 1973.

Contract: 3◊. Lead ♣6.

In point of fact Gérard Desrousseaux was endplayed before his first lead, but he thought that it would be a reasonable thing to lead the ♣6. Now, had declarer followed the principle that three cards can take the ♣9, but only one the king, he might, conceivably, have made his contract by putting up the king. However, he did not like the idea of sacrificing it to East's supposed ace—he ducked. Thus East won the trick with the ♣J and then switched to the ♡J, which was allowed to run to dummy's queen. The ♠Q from dummy was taken by East who continued in hearts. As declarer, too, had to lose another trump trick he went down one.

Solution Number 75

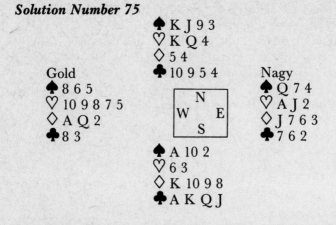

```
                    ♠ K J 9 3
                    ♡ K Q 4
                    ◇ 5 4
                    ♣ 10 9 5 4
Gold                                    Nagy
♠ 8 6 5              ┌─────────┐        ♠ Q 7 4
♡ 10 9 8 7 5        │    N    │        ♡ A J 2
◇ A Q 2             │ W     E │        ◇ J 7 6 3
♣ 8 3               │    S    │        ♣ 7 6 2
                    └─────────┘
                    ♠ A 10 2
                    ♡ 6 3
                    ◇ K 10 9 8
                    ♣ A K Q J
```

Canadian Olympic Trials at Ste. Agathe, Quebec, 1971.
Contract: 3 No Trumps. Lead ♡10.

East took dummy's queen with the ace and continued in that suit. Declarer won the third round with the ♡K, then cashed his four top clubs. West discarded the ◇2 on the third club. At this point it might be opportune to show East's cards and to ask what East and West discarded on the fourth club. Sam Gold threw the ♡9 and Peter Nagy the ♠4.

By doing this in co-operation they fooled declarer beautifully into taking the losing spade finesse for it looked as if Gold had been forced to throw a good heart to keep the ♠Q guarded. The trick was successful—declarer cashed the ♠A and let the ♠10 run. Nagy won and switched to a diamond, and the contract went down two.

At the other table declarer finessed spades the correct way in the fourth trick, which all goes to prove that, sometimes, it is wise to make an early decision and not to give your opponents any chance to fool you!

♡

Deal Number 76

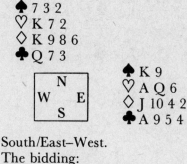

♠ 7 3 2
♡ K 7 2
◇ K 9 8 6
♣ Q 7 3

♠ K 9
♡ A Q 6
◇ J 10 4 2
♣ A 9 5 4

South/East–West.
The bidding:

South	North
1 ♠	1 NT
2 ♠	

West leads the ♡10. Dummy follows with the ♡2. How does East plan the defence?

Deal Number 77

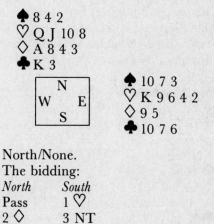

♠ 8 4 2
♡ Q J 10 8
◇ A 8 4 3
♣ K 3

♠ 10 7 3
♡ K 9 6 4 2
◇ 9 5
♣ 10 7 6

North/None.
The bidding:

North	South
Pass	1 ♡
2 ◇	3 NT
4 ♡	

West leads the ◇Q. Declarer wins with dummy's ace to play the ♡Q, covered by East and taken by declarer, West being void. Declarer plays the ♣A, takes the ♣Q over with the ♣K, plays the ◇3 to the king in the closed hand and continues with the ◇6 to West's jack. What card does East play?

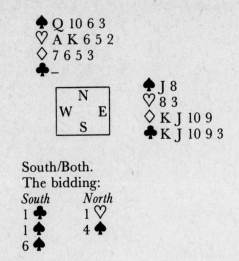

♠ Q 10 6 3
♡ A K 6 5 2
◇ 7 6 5 3
♣ –

♠ J 8
♡ 8 3
◇ K J 10 9
♣ K J 10 9 3

South/Both.
The bidding:

South	North
1 ♣	1 ♡
1 ♠	4 ♠
6 ♠	

West leads the ♡Q. Declarer wins with dummy's king and plays a diamond to the queen in the closed hand. He draws the ♣A, throwing a diamond from dummy and ruffs a club with the ♠3. A diamond is played to the ace to ruff another club with the ♠6. On the ♡A he discards the ◇4 and then plays the ♡2 from dummy. What card does East play?

Solution Number 76

♠ 7 3 2
♡ K 7 2
◇ K 9 8 6
♣ Q 7 3

Kaitera
♠ 10 6 4
♡ 10 9 8 4 3
◇ 7 3
♣ K J 10

Lindén
♠ K 9
♡ A Q 6
◇ J 10 4 2
♣ A 9 5 4

♠ A Q J 8 5
♡ J 5
◇ A Q 5
♣ 8 6 2

Nordic Ladies' Championships at Noresund, Norway, 1975. Finland-Sweden.

Contract: 2♠. Lead ♡10.

Finland's Mrs Lindén won the trick with the ♡Q and switched to the ♣4. Mrs Kaitera won with the king and continued with the ♣J. East took dummy's queen with the ace and returned the ♣5 to West's ♣10. Mrs Kaitera switched back to hearts, and when Mrs Lindén won with the ace and played the thirteenth club, West's ♠10 became good for the undertrick.

Solution Number 77

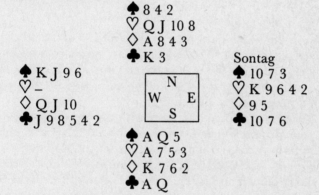

♠ 8 4 2
♡ Q J 10 8
◇ A 8 4 3
♣ K 3

♠ K J 9 6
♡ –
◇ Q J 10
♣ J 9 8 5 4 2

Sontag
♠ 10 7 3
♡ K 9 6 4 2
◇ 9 5
♣ 10 7 6

♠ A Q 5
♡ A 7 5 3
◇ K 7 6 2
♣ A Q

The Vanderbilt Cup at Atlanta, spring 1971.

Contract: 4♡. Lead ◇Q.

Declarer won with dummy's ace to play the ♡Q, which East covered with the king and declarer took with the ♡A. He cashed the ♣A, took the ♣Q over with dummy's king, played the ◇3 to the king and a third diamond to West's ◇J. Alan Sontag ruffed his partner's trick with the ♡2 thus being able to switch to the ♠10!

As a consequence declarer had to lose two spades to West and went down one, Sontag's ♡9 still being good for a trick.

At the other table the play went in the same way until the sixth trick, when East discarded a spade. West was endplayed and the contract was made.

Solution Number 78

```
              ♠ Q 10 6 3
              ♡ A K 6 5 2
              ◇ 7 6 5 3
              ♣ —                    McWilliams
♠ K 5 2                              ♠ J 8
♡ Q J 10 9 4      ┌─────────┐        ♡ 8 3
◇ 8 2             │    N    │        ◇ K J 10 9
♣ 7 4 2          │ W     E │        ♣ K J 10 9 3
                 │    S    │
                 └─────────┘
              ♠ A 9 7 4
              ♡ 7
              ◇ A Q 4
              ♣ A Q 8 6 5
```

Rubber Bridge in USA, 1962.

Contract: 6♠. Lead ♡Q.

Declarer won with dummy's ace, finessed in diamonds with the queen, cashed the ♣A throwing a diamond from dummy, ruffed a club with the ♠3, went home on the ◇A to ruff another club with the ♠6. On the ♡K he got rid of his last diamond, and then played the ♡2 from dummy.

Bill McWilliams forced declarer with the ♠8. Declarer had to overruff with the ♠9 and ruffed a club with the ♠10. On the ♡5 from dummy McWilliams made his second uppercut with the ♠J, which cost declarer's ace of trumps. With three cards left declarer played his last club. West had to ruff with the ♠2 and was then overruffed with dummy's last trump—the queen. It was thanks to McWilliams' double uppercut that West's ♠K and lowly ♠5 had become a tenace over declarer's ♠7-4, and thus the contract went one down.

A similar double uppercut was carried out by Harry Fishbein in the 'Summer Nationals' (men's pairs) in Chicago, 1949.

Deal Number 79

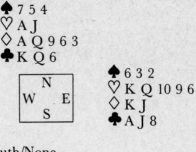

♠ 7 5 4
♡ A J
♢ A Q 9 6 3
♣ K Q 6

♠ 6 3 2
♡ K Q 10 9 6
♢ K J
♣ A J 8

South/None.
The bidding:

South	North
Pass	1 NT
2 ♠	

West leads the ♡5. Declarer wins with dummy's ace and plays the ♠4 to the queen in the closed hand, taken by West with the king. West switches to the ♣9 which is covered with dummy's ♣Q. How does East plan the defence now and later?

Deal Number 80

♠ A K 6
♡ A 8 5 3
♢ 10 7 3
♣ K 6 4

♠ J 7 5
♡ 7
♢ J 6 5 2
♣ A J 10 9 5

North/North–South with partscore 60.
The bidding:

North	East	South	West
1 ♣	Double	1 NT	2♢
Pass	Pass	2 NT	

West leads the ♠5. Declarer wins with dummy's king and plays the ♣4 to the queen in the closed hand. How does West plan the defence?

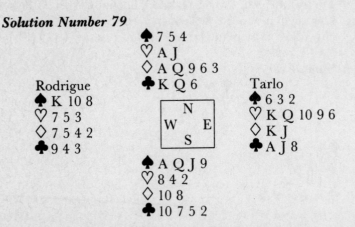

♠ 7 6 3
♡ 9 6
◇ K Q J 9 6 4
♣ A 6

♠ K 10 5 2
♡ A 5 3
◇ A 7 2
♣ K 5 3

North/Both.
The bidding:

North	South
3 ◇	3 NT

West leads the ♡J. How does East plan the defence?

Solution Number 79

♠ 7 5 4
♡ A J
◇ A Q 9 6 3
♣ K Q 6

Rodrigue
♠ K 10 8
♡ 7 5 3
◇ 7 5 4 2
♣ 9 4 3

Tarlo
♠ 6 3 2
♡ K Q 10 9 6
◇ K J
♣ A J 8

♠ A Q J 9
♡ 8 4 2
◇ 10 8
♣ 10 7 5 2

European Championships at Dublin, 1967. Great Britain-Lebanon.

Contract: 2♠. Lead ♡5.

Declarer won with dummy's ace to try the trump finesse with the ♠Q. Claude Rodrigue won with the ♠K and switched to the ♣9. Declarer covered with dummy's ♣Q, and Louis Tarlo ducked with the ♣8! Declarer decided to draw one more round of trumps before he led a heart. Tarlo won with the ♡Q and removed dummy's last trump. Then declarer played the ◊10 and let it run. Tarlo thought that now was the time to try that old trick—he won with the ◊K and played the ♡10. Declarer, ruffing with his last trump swallowed the bait hook line and sinker, and took the deep diamond finesse. Since he had, in the meantime, thrown dummy's clubs in the expectation of taking the rest in diamonds, declarer won no more tricks, going down three.

Solution Number 80

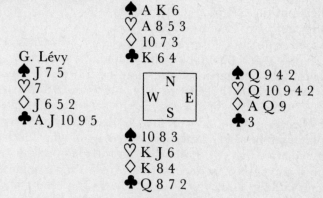

G. Lévy

North:
♠ A K 6
♡ A 8 5 3
◊ 10 7 3
♣ K 6 4

West:
♠ J 7 5
♡ 7
◊ J 6 5 2
♣ A J 10 9 5

East:
♠ Q 9 4 2
♡ Q 10 9 4 2
◊ A Q 9
♣ 3

South:
♠ 10 8 3
♡ K J 6
◊ K 8 4
♣ Q 8 7 2

Rubber Bridge at Lyon, France, 1969.
Contract: 2 No Trumps. Lead ♣5.
Declarer considered the position coming to the conclusion that he needed two club tricks. He decided to play for the doubleton ace in East. Therefore he won with dummy's ♠K and then played the ♣4 to the queen. Nobody will ever know whether Doctor Lévy was a mind-reader, but, in any event, he was only too well aware of declarer's strategy. So he dropped the ♣5 under the queen, and when declarer continued with the ♣7 Lévy followed with the ♣9. In accordance with his plan declarer ducked in dummy. He had the shock of his life when Lévy then cashed three more club tricks before he switched back to spades, the inevitable result was that the contract went down two.

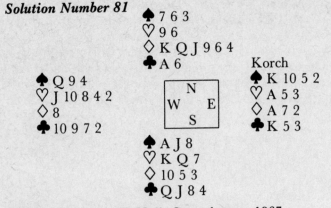

```
              ♠ 7 6 3
              ♡ 9 6
              ◊ K Q J 9 6 4
              ♣ A 6
                                    Korch
  ♠ Q 9 4            N          ♠ K 10 5 2
  ♡ J 10 8 4 2  W       E       ♡ A 5 3
  ◊ 8               S            ◊ A 7 2
  ♣ 10 9 7 2                     ♣ K 5 3
              ♠ A J 8
              ♡ K Q 7
              ◊ 10 5 3
              ♣ Q J 8 4
```

Duplicate in the KB Hall, Copenhagen, 1967.

Contract: 3 No Trumps. Lead ♡J.

As soon as he saw dummy's cards Morten A. Korch realised immediately that he could block the diamonds, and that it was of the utmost importance to knock out the side entry. This he did by winning with the ♡A and switching to the ♣K. Declarer won and played the ◊K, dropping the ◊10 from the closed hand when West followed with the ◊8. Korch was no wiser by this play, but for safety's sake he ducked again when declarer continued with the ◊Q. From then on the diamond suit was hopeless, and declarer seized the chance of leading a spade and finessing with the jack. West won with the ♠Q and continued in hearts—declarer could not make more than eight tricks in all.

It will be well known that this defence is called a 'Merrimac Coup', but what may not be known is that is its named after the cruiser 'Merrimac', which the Americans sank in the port of Santiago to blockade the Spanish fleet. It is not amongst the rarest of coups. The last that I have heard of was in the final of the Pairs Championships at Silkeborg in Denmark in February, 1972 and this was when Asger Soerensen successfully carried it out. Further back in 1963 the German Fritz Chodziesner executed it (and, indeed, in the opening lead) in a Belgium-Germany match. Even much earlier, in 1932, Oswald Jacoby achieved the coup in a duplicate in the United States, to repeat it in 1963.

Deal Number 82

♠ A 8 4 3
♡ –
♦ Q 8 6
♣ A J 10 8 7 5

♠ K
♡ J 10 9 8 7 5 2
♦ K 4
♣ K 3 2

South/Both.
The bidding:

South	West	North	East
Pass	2 ♡	Double	Pass
3 NT			

West leads the ♡J. Declarer wins with the king and takes a club finesse whith the ♣10. East wins with the queen and switches to the ♠7. West's ♠K is allowed to hold the trick. How does West proceed?

Deal Number 83

♠ K 5
♡ A 7 5 2
♦ A K 10 9 8 5
♣ K

♠ 9 7
♡ K 6 3
♦ J 6 2
♣ A Q 7 6 2

North/Both.
The bidding:

North	South
1 ♦	1 ♡
4 ♡	

West leads the ♣4. How does East plan the defence?

119

Deal Number 84

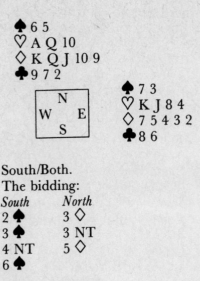

♠ 6 5
♡ A Q 10
♢ K Q J 10 9
♣ 9 7 2

♠ 7 3
♡ K J 8 4
♢ 7 5 4 3 2
♣ 8 6

South/Both.
The bidding:

South	North
2 ♠	3 ♢
3 ♠	3 NT
4 NT	5 ♢
6 ♠	

West leads the ♡2 and declarer finesses with dummy's ♡Q. How does East plan the defence?

Solution Number 82

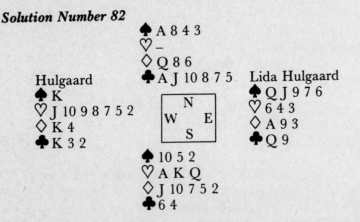

♠ A 8 4 3
♡ –
♢ Q 8 6
♣ A J 10 8 7 5

Hulgaard
♠ K
♡ J 10 9 8 7 5 2
♢ K 4
♣ K 3 2

Lida Hulgaard
♠ Q J 9 7 6
♡ 6 4 3
♢ A 9 3
♣ Q 9

♠ 10 5 2
♡ A K Q
♢ J 10 7 5 2
♣ 6 4

Team Matches in Copenhagen between five teams from four countries, June 1973. Denmark-Sweden.

Contract: 3NT. Lead ♡J.

Declarer won with the ♡K, and then played the ♣4 to dummy's ♣10. Winning with the queen Lida Hulgaard at once realised that it would be unwise to return partner's suit, partly because it might give declarer some heart tricks which could otherwise be blocked, and partly as it would give him the possibility of another club finesse. So she switched to the ♠7. Johs. Hulgaard was allowed to hold the trick with the ♠K. He, too, was well aware of what was going on and so he switched to the—◇K. When he continued with the ◇4 declarer put up dummy's queen, but it was far too late—he should have unblocked the queen under the king. Now Lida Hulgaard ducked and declarer's only possibility was then to play clubs from the top hoping that West would be endplayed on the ♣K with only hearts left. But Johs. Hulgaard was very wideawake and unblocked the ♣K with the result that Lida Hulgaard took the last two tricks, and the contract went down two.

Solution Number 83

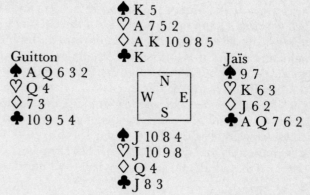

```
                    ♠ K 5
                    ♡ A 7 5 2
                    ◇ A K 10 9 8 5
                    ♣ K
Guitton                              Jaïs
♠ A Q 6 3 2          ┌─────────┐     ♠ 9 7
♡ Q 4                │    N    │     ♡ K 6 3
◇ 7 3              W │         │ E   ◇ J 6 2
♣ 10 9 5 4           │    S    │     ♣ A Q 7 6 2
                     └─────────┘
                    ♠ J 10 8 4
                    ♡ J 10 9 8
                    ◇ Q 4
                    ♣ J 8 3
```

European Championships, 1973. France-Lebanon.
    Contract: 4♡. Lead ♣4.
    Pierre Jaïs took the king with the ace and switched to the ♠9. Charles Guitton went up with the ace and continued with the ♠2 to dummy's king. Declarer entered the closed hand with the ◇Q to finesse trumps and Jaïs, winning with the ♡K, now played the ◇J! Dummy won, and had declarer then laid down the ♡A things would have been clear. But as he counted on split trump honours, and as the ◇J looked like a doubleton, he tried to enter the closed hand through a diamond ruff. Guitton overruffed with the blank ♡Q, and the contract went down one.

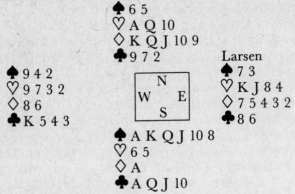

European Championships, 1949. Norway-Iceland.

Contract: 6♠. Lead ♡2.

Robert Larsen took dummy's queen with the king and tried to picture declarer's hand in his mind. With the ten diamonds he could see he found it not at all improbable that declarer held the blank ace and it was important, therefore, to remove dummy's entry. West's lead might be an indication that South held a doubleton heart, and so Larsen played a heart back into dummy's tenace! Now declarer was forced to use the diamonds while he was in dummy. He was smart enough to unblock the ◊A on a third round of hearts, for by doing this he could try to cash three diamonds and discard three clubs. However, West ruffed the third diamond, and so the contract went one down.

Deal Number 85

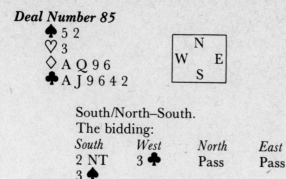

♠ 5 2
♡ 3
◇ A Q 9 6
♣ A J 9 6 4 2

South/North–South.
The bidding:

South	West	North	East
2 NT	3 ♣	Pass	Pass
3 ♠			

What card should West lead?

Deal Number 86

♠ J 8 7
♡ A 9 5
◇ K 9 6 4
♣ A Q 4

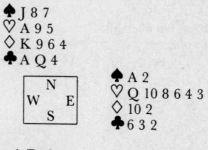

♠ A 2
♡ Q 10 8 6 4 3
◇ 10 2
♣ 6 3 2

South/Both.
The bidding:

South	North
1 ♠	2 ♣
2 ◇	2 ♡
2 NT	3 NT

West leads the ♡J. Dummy follows with the ♡5. How does East plan the defence?

Deal Number 87

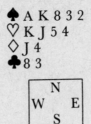

♠ A K 8 3 2
♡ K J 5 4
◇ J 4
♣ 8 3

♠ Q J 10 6
♡ 7 3
◇ K 5 2
♣ J 9 6 4

```
      N
   W     E
      S
```

South/East–West.
The bidding:

South	North
1 ◇	2 ♠
3 ♡	4 ♡

West leads the ♣4. East wins the ♣K and A, declarer following
with the ♣10 and Q, and switches to the ◇Q. Declarer wins
with the ◇A, West following with the ◇5 and dummy with the
◇4. Declarer draws the three top hearts, East following, and
then plays the ◇3. How does West plan the defence from here?

Solution Number 85

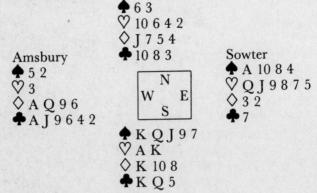

♠ 6 3
♡ 10 6 4 2
◇ J 7 5 4
♣ 10 8 3

Amsbury
♠ 5 2
♡ 3
◇ A Q 9 6
♣ A J 9 6 4 2

```
      N
   W     E
      S
```

Sowter
♠ A 10 8 4
♡ Q J 9 8 7 5
◇ 3 2
♣ 7

♠ K Q J 9 7
♡ A K
◇ K 10 8
♣ K Q 5

The Camrose Trial. Great Britain, 1978.
    Contract: 3♠. Lead ♣A.
Joe Amsbury chose the lead of the ♣A and, summing up

from the bidding that declarer held the ♣K-Q, he continued
with the ♣2 for East to ruff. Tony Sowter promptly switched to
the ◇3 and, winning with the queen, Amsbury gave partner
another club ruff. The ◇2 to the ace gave Amsbury the opportunity to hand on a plate to his partner a diamond ruff, and now
Sowter switched to the ♡Q. Declarer won and hurried to play a
trump but, winning with the ♠A, Sowter was still able to give
Amsbury a heart ruff. The contract went four down.

Solution Number 86

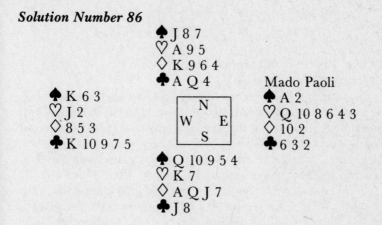

```
                    ♠ J 8 7
                    ♡ A 9 5
                    ◇ K 9 6 4
                    ♣ A Q 4
                                        Mado Paoli
  ♠ K 6 3              N               ♠ A 2
  ♡ J 2            W       E           ♡ Q 10 8 6 4 3
  ◇ 8 5 3              S               ◇ 10 2
  ♣ K 10 9 7 5                         ♣ 6 3 2
                    ♠ Q 10 9 5 4
                    ♡ K 7
                    ◇ A Q J 7
                    ♣ J 8
```

France, 1974.
    Contract: 3 No Trumps. Lead ♡J.
    The lead looked too good to be true, for if West held the ♠K
he would try to come first on lead to continue in hearts, and
thus save East's eventual ♠A. But what would happen if
declarer should duck, which naturally, he would do? In that
event East-West would get only the one heart trick. So Mado
Paoli took the ♡J over with the queen and was allowed to hold
the trick, as could well be expected. Bravely she switched to
clubs, with the consequence that West's ♣9 forced dummy's
queen. Declarer played the ♠7 from dummy, and now Mado
Paoli rushed to win the first spade trick so that she could
continue in clubs. The inevitable result was that declarer now
had to cash his tricks in the red suits so that he could go only one
down.

125

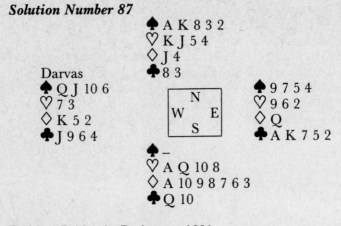

♠ A K 8 3 2
♡ K J 5 4
◇ J 4
♣ 8 3

Darvas
♠ Q J 10 6
♡ 7 3
◇ K 5 2
♣ J 9 6 4

♠ 9 7 5 4
♡ 9 6 2
◇ Q
♣ A K 7 5 2

♠ —
♡ A Q 10 8
◇ A 10 9 8 7 6 3
♣ Q 10

Rubber Bridge in Budapest, 1931.

Contract: 4♡. Lead ♣4.

East cashed the two top clubs and switched to the ◇Q. Declarer won with the ◇A, and if Robert Darvas had now been South he would have unblocked dummy's jack. But the actual South was not so farseeing—he followed with dummy's ◇4. After three rounds of trumps, with Darvas dropping the ♣9, declarer led a low diamond, and Darvas ducked! Dummy's ◇J had to win the trick, and with that the long diamonds were blocked. So declarer led the ♠2 from dummy and discarded a diamond from the closed hand. East covered with the ♠7, but for safety's sake Darvas took it with the ♠10. If, for instance, East had held the trick and should have played another spade then declarer could ruff, and dummy would be high. And if Darvas should play the ◇K then dummy could ruff, and the closed hand would be good.

So Darvas played the ♣J. The best declarer could do now was to discard a spade from dummy, ruff in the closed hand, and then ruff a diamond, cash the ♠A and K, lose the last spade, and go down one.

Deal Number 88

        ♠ A 10 9 8 7 2
        ♡ Q J
        ♢ A J 7
        ♣ J 8

♠ Q 6 5 4
♡ 10 8 7
♢ 8 3
♣ Q 9 6 5

South/North–South.
The bidding:

South	North
1 NT	3 ♠
3 NT	

West leads the ♣5. Declarer wins the trick with dummy's ♣J and plays the ♠2 to the ♠J in the closed hand. How does West plan the defence?

Deal Number 89

        ♠ 10 9 4 2
        ♡ Q 5 4 3
        ♢ Q 4 3
        ♣ 7 4

♠ J
♡ K 8 6
♢ A K 9 7 5
♣ J 9 6 5

South/Both.
The bidding:

South	North
2 ♢+)	2 ♡
3 ♣	3 ♢
3 ♠	4 ♠

+) A strong hand with three four-card-suits and a singleton diamond.

West leads the ♠J. Declarer wins with the ♠Q and plays the ♢J. How does West plan the defence?

127

Deal Number 90

        ♠ Q
        ♡ A Q 8 5 3 2
        ◇ J 10 9
        ♣ J 10 8

♠ A K 3
♡ K 10 9 6 4
◇ A 4
♣ K 6 2

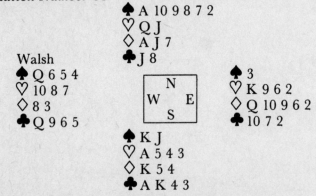

West/None.
The bidding:

West	North	East	South
1 ♡	Pass	Pass	2 ♡
Double	3 ♡	4 ♠	5 ◇
Double			

West leads the ♠K, East following with the ♠2. How does West continue?

Solution Number 88

        ♠ A 10 9 8 7 2
        ♡ Q J
        ◇ A J 7
Walsh   ♣ J 8

♠ Q 6 5 4   ♠ 3
♡ 10 8 7   ♡ K 9 6 2
◇ 8 3   ◇ Q 10 9 6 2
♣ Q 9 6 5   ♣ 10 7 2

        ♠ K J
        ♡ A 5 4 3
        ◇ K 5 4
        ♣ A K 4 3

The Vanderbilt Cup at Cleveland, March 1969.
   Contract: 3 No Trumps. Lead ♣5.
   On first appearance the lead, going to dummy's ♣J, seemed to be unlucky. However, declarer mistakenly used this entry to play a spade and to finesse with the ♠J. Richard Walsh ducked this.

Declarer then cashed the ♠K. If he had had any suspicion of the spade distribution it would have been quite a good idea to have taken it over with the ace, and then to continue with the ♠10. With the ◇A as entry to the remaining spades and the heart finesse twelve tricks would then be made, as had happened at the other table. But there South had not been put to the test, as West, with the same declarer's play, took the ♠J with the ♠Q.

Here, however, declarer now needed two entries to be able to make full use of the spades, and one of them had to be established by playing low hearts to dummy. The result was that declarer had to lose a heart trick, and only made eleven tricks.

Solution Number 89

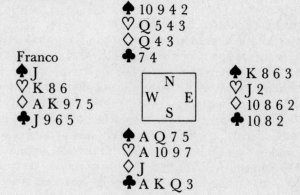

Teams-of-four Championship in Italy, 1970.
Contract: 4♠.
Following the intricate but precise style of Italian bidding everyone could be only too well aware that South held three four-card suits and a singleton diamond.

Arturo Franco led the ♠J. Declarer won with the ♠Q and switched to the ◇J. Franco won with the ◇K and then switched to the ♡6! Declarer could not imagine that, after the bidding, anyone could have the courage to lead away from the ♡K. So he ducked in dummy, having to take East's ♡J with the ace. When declarer then drew the ♠A he was lost. East won the next spade with the king, and then played the ♡2. Franco won with the king to give East a heart ruff, and the contract was down one.

Solution Number 90

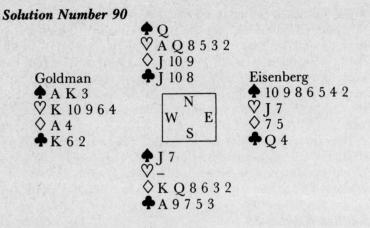

```
                    ♠ Q
                    ♡ A Q 8 5 3 2
                    ◇ J 10 9
Goldman             ♣ J 10 8           Eisenberg
♠ A K 3                                ♠ 10 9 8 6 5 4 2
♡ K 10 9 6 4         ┌─────────┐       ♡ J 7
◇ A 4                │    N    │       ◇ 7 5
♣ K 6 2              │ W     E │       ♣ Q 4
                     │    S    │
                     └─────────┘
                    ♠ J 7
                    ♡ –
                    ◇ K Q 8 6 3 2
                    ♣ A 9 7 5 3
```

Teams-of-four in USA, 1969.

Contract: 5◇ doubled. Lead ♣K.

Here was a typical demonstration of the Lavinthal signal. Dummy's singleton spade on the lead of the ♠K gave East the chance to show preference for either hearts or clubs. For example, should he be void in hearts he would follow with the ♠10, but William Eisenberg chose to drop the ♠2 with the consequence that Robert Goldman switched to the ♣2. Then, declarer took Eisenberg's ♣Q with the ace and at once played the ◇2. Goldman was quick to go up with the ◇A, to play the ♣K, and to continue with the ♣6. Eisenberg got his last trump with a ruff—that being necessary to set the contract twice.

Deal Number 91

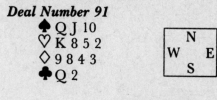

♠ Q J 10
♡ K 8 5 2
♢ 9 8 4 3
♣ Q 2

North/Both.
The bidding:

North	South
1 ♢	2 ♣
4 ♣	6 ♣

What does West lead after this bidding?

Deal Number 92

♠ J 10 3
♡ K 7 3
♢ A Q 10 6 5
♣ 9 2

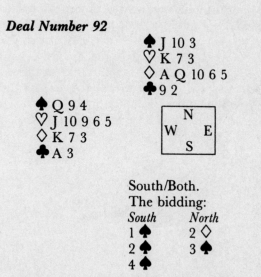

♠ Q 9 4
♡ J 10 9 6 5
♢ K 7 3
♣ A 3

South/Both.
The bidding:

South	North
1 ♠	2 ♢
2 ♠	3 ♠
4 ♠	

West leads the ♡J. Declarer wins with dummy's king to lead the ♣2. East wins the trick with the ♣J and switches to the ♠6. Declarer wins with the ♠K and plays the ♣6 which West must take with the ace. What card does West play now?

131

Deal Number 93

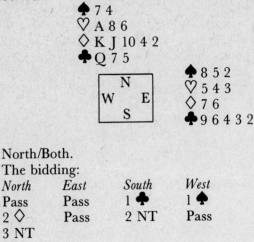

♠ 7 4
♡ A 8 6
◇ K J 10 4 2
♣ Q 7 5

♠ 8 5 2
♡ 5 4 3
◇ 7 6
♣ 9 6 4 3 2

North/Both.
The bidding:

North	East	South	West
Pass	Pass	1 ♣	1 ♠
2 ◇	Pass	2 NT	Pass
3 NT			

It must be stated that during the deal North unintentionally exposed East's ♡3, but no time was wasted on redealing. West leads the ♡K and dummy ducks. What card does East play?

Solution Number 91

♠ A 3
♡ J 10
◇ A K J 5
♣ J 9 7 6 5

del Duca
♠ Q J 10
♡ K 8 5 2
◇ 9 8 4 3
♣ Q 2

♠ 8 7 5 4 2
♡ Q 7 6
◇ Q 7 6
♣ 10 3

♠ K 9 6
♡ A 9 4 3
◇ 10 2
♣ A K 8 4

Golfer's Club, Paris, 1966.
   Contract: 6♣.
   Cino del Duca led the ♣2!

132

Declarer covered with dummy's ♣9 and took East's ♣10 with the king. As nobody of course leads from a doubleton trump queen declarer took it as being certain that East held the ♠Q and led the ♠6 to dummy's ace, to take the trump finesse. Del Duca got his blank queen, exited in spades, and then waited patiently for the undertrick in hearts.

Solution Number 92

```
                    ♠ J 10 3
                    ♡ K 7 3
                    ◊ A Q 10 6 5
                    ♣ 9 2
Jannersten
♠ Q 9 4                              ♠ 6 5
♡ J 10 9 6 5      ┌─────────┐        ♡ 4 2
◊ K 7 3           │    N    │        ◊ J 9 8 4 2
♣ A 3             │ W     E │        ♣ K Q J 4
                  │    S    │
                  └─────────┘
                    ♠ A K 8 7 2
                    ♡ A Q 8
                    ◊ —
                    ♣ 10 8 7 6 5
```

Stockholm, 1950.

Contract: 4 ♠. Lead ♡J.

Declarer won with dummy's king and played the ♣2. East won the trick with the ♣J and switched to the ♠6. Declarer won with the ♠K and continued with the ♣6 which West had to take with the ♣A.

If West should now play a red card declarer would gain the time to ruff two clubs; if West should play a low trump declarer would then get for certain only one ruff, but would lose no trump trick. Eric Jannersten hit upon the killing lead—the ♠Q! Declarer could now win the ace, *but* the ruff would have to be made with dummy's ♠J with the result that Jannersten's ♠9 took a trick, instead of the queen. Declarer could throw one club on the ◊A, but he had to lose the fifth club to East.

133

$\spadesuit$ 7 4
$\heartsuit$ A 8 6
$\diamondsuit$ K J 10 4 2
$\clubsuit$ Q 7 5

$\spadesuit$ Q J 10 6 3
$\heartsuit$ K Q 10 9 7
$\diamondsuit$ A 9
$\clubsuit$ 8

Dick Frey
$\spadesuit$ 8 5 2
$\heartsuit$ 5 4 3
$\diamondsuit$ 7 6
$\clubsuit$ 9 6 4 3 2

$\spadesuit$ A K 9
$\heartsuit$ J 2
$\diamondsuit$ Q 8 5 3
$\clubsuit$ A K J 10

Rubber Bridge in the train home from New York City.
Contract: 3 No Trumps. Lead $\heartsuit$K.

Richard L. Frey amusingly told how he was asked, when commuting from New York City, to be a fourth in an established rubber missing a member. But as North had lost and, during the dealing, had shown the $\heartsuit$3, Dick Frey said that he thought the cards should be redealt. He was told, however, by his travelling companions that they never troubled to redeal unless the card shown was an honour. The result, of course, was that Dick had to make the best of it with East's poor hand.

Sometimes, however, there is a rough justice in this world, and when declarer played dummy's $\heartsuit$6 to West's king, Dick's reply was to drop the $\heartsuit$4. Everyone was perfectly well aware that he held the $\heartsuit$3, so West came to the conclusion that he had tried to show three hearts. As a result West continued with the $\heartsuit$Q, dropping declarer's jack, so that he could continue in hearts. Declarer could not take more than seven tricks without diamonds, and so he went two down.

Deal Number 94

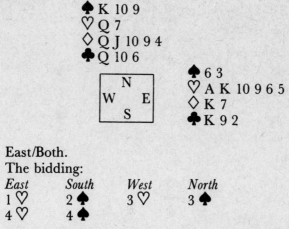

♠ K 10 9
♡ Q 7
◇ Q J 10 9 4
♣ Q 10 6

♠ 6 3
♡ A K 10 9 6 5
◇ K 7
♣ K 9 2

East/Both.
The bidding:

East	South	West	North
1 ♡	2 ♠	3 ♡	3 ♠
4 ♡	4 ♠		

West leads the ♡3. How does East plan the defence?

Deal Number 95

♠ K J 5
♡ 10 8 3
◇ A Q 10 9 8 2
♣ 7

♠ 4 3
♡ K J 9 6 4 2
◇ K 4
♣ K 8 3

West/None.
The bidding:

West	North	East	South
1 ♣	1 ◇	1 ♡	1 ♠
Pass	2 ♠	4 ♡	4 ♠
Pass	Pass	Double	

West opens with the ♡A and continues with the ♡7. Declarer ruffs and plays the ◇6 to dummy's ◇8. How does East plan the defence?

Deal Number 96

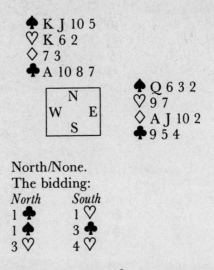

♠ K J 10 5
♡ K 6 2
◇ 7 3
♣ A 10 8 7

♠ Q 6 3 2
♡ 9 7
◇ A J 10 2
♣ 9 5 4

North/None.
The bidding:

North	South
1 ♣	1 ♡
1 ♠	3 ♣
3 ♡	4 ♡

West leads the ◇5. East wins with the ◇A and returns the ◇2. Declarer wins with the king and plays trumps. West wins the second round with the ♡A. He switches to the ♣3. Declarer wins with the ♣K and draws West's last trump. What card does East discard?

Solution Number 94

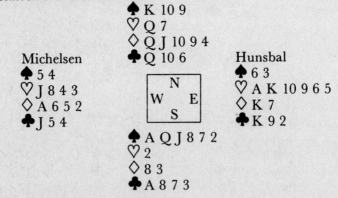

♠ K 10 9
♡ Q 7
◇ Q J 10 9 4
♣ Q 10 6

Michelsen
♠ 5 4
♡ J 8 4 3
◇ A 6 5 2
♣ J 5 4

Hunsbal
♠ 6 3
♡ A K 10 9 6 5
◇ K 7
♣ K 9 2

♠ A Q J 8 7 2
♡ 2
◇ 8 3
♣ A 8 7 3

Teams-of-four, in Copenhagen, 1958.
Contract: 4♠. Lead ♡3.
Finn Hunsbal went up with the ♡A to indicate to his partner

136

that there was nothing more of any advantage in that suit. He could clearly see that from his raise Erik Michelsen must, at least, be holding the ◇A. But the logical question was from where the fourth trick could come. The only reasonable answer was that Erik must be holding as high as the ♣J, for then a club trick might well be established before dummy's long diamonds were set up. Ever alert for a suit switch Finn lost no time on the hearts, but at once switched to the ♣2.

Erik Michelsen held, in fact, the ♣J, which cost dummy's queen. Declarer, having drawn the trumps, played the ◇3. At once Erik went up with the ace, to switch to the ♣5, and Finn's ♣K was set up, while the diamonds were still being stopped by the king.

Solution Number 95

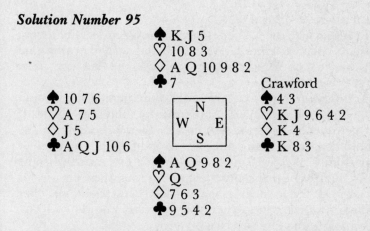

International Match about 1960. Great Britain-USA.

Contract: 4♠ doubled. Lead ♡A.

Declarer ruffed the next heart and played the ◇6 to dummy's ◇8.

Your guess is right! John Crawford followed with the ◇4. It was now that declarer backed diamonds with everything he had, and drew three rounds of trumps to finesse diamonds again. West's ◇J strengthened his confidence that West also held the king. However, Crawford took the queen with his blank king and then switched to clubs. And so the contract went down three.

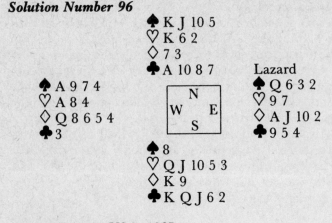

```
                    ♠ K J 10 5
                    ♡ K 6 2
                    ◇ 7 3
                    ♣ A 10 8 7            Lazard
    ♠ A 9 7 4          ┌─────────┐       ♠ Q 6 3 2
    ♡ A 8 4            │    N    │       ♡ 9 7
    ◇ Q 8 6 5 4      W │ W     E │ E     ◇ A J 10 2
    ♣ 3                │    S    │       ♣ 9 5 4
                       └─────────┘
                    ♠ 8
                    ♡ Q J 10 5 3
                    ◇ K 9
                    ♣ K Q J 6 2
```

Master Pairs in USA, 1967.

Contract: 4♡. Lead ◇5.

East won with the ◇A and returned the ◇2 to declarer's king. Declarer played trumps. West won the second trump and switched to the ♣3. Declarer won with the ♣A and drew West's last trump.

At this point Sidney Lazard could count that declarer would be holding five clubs and, consequently, only one spade. If partner should have the ♠A it was therefore vital that he should be warned not to duck but to go up with it on the first opportunity. West was given the warning by Lazard when he threw the ♠Q on the third trump! It was then no use for declarer to try to steal a spade trick. West could see that nothing now could be achieved by waiting, and the contract was made without an overtrick.

But should it have been a duplicate for average players the contract would have gone down. Mrs Jones would open with the ♣3, go up with the ♠A or ♡A in the next trick, and then switch to the ◇4. Mr Jones would win with the ◇A and give her a club ruff, and his wife would then cash her second ace.

Deal Number 97

♠ A J 4
♥ K 10
♦ A 10 4 3
♣ A Q 10 6

♠ Q 10 3
♥ 7 6
♦ 8 6 5
♣ K J 8 3 2

```
      N
   W     E
      S
```

North/Both.
The bidding:

North	East	South	West
1 ♣	1 ♦	1 ♥	Pass
1 NT	Pass	4 ♥	

West leads the ♦8. After the ♦A and three rounds of trumps declarer plays the ♣2 to dummy's ♣J and continues with the ♣A. How does West plan the defence?

Deal Number 98

♠ 9 7
♥ Q 7 4
♦ K 7 2
♣ A K J 9 3

♠ A
♥ 9 8 5
♦ J 6 3
♣ Q 8 7 6 5 4

```
      N
   W     E
      S
```

North/Both.
The bidding:

North	East	South	West
1 ♣	Pass	2 ♦	3 ♠
4 ♦	Pass	4 NT	5 ♠
5 NT	Pass	6 ♦	

West leads the ♣2. Declarer drops the ♣K under East's ace. What is East's next lead?

139

Deal Number 99

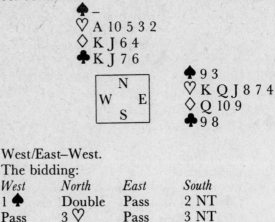

♠ –
♡ A 10 5 3 2
◊ K J 6 4
♣ K J 7 6

♠ 9 3
♡ K Q J 8 7 4
◊ Q 10 9
♣ 9 8

West/East–West.
The bidding:

West	North	East	South
1 ♠	Double	Pass	2 NT
Pass	3 ♡	Pass	3 NT

West leads the ♣3. Declarer wins with the ♣Q in the closed hand and continues with the ♣4 to dummy's jack in order to play the ♡2 from dummy. How does East plan the defence?

Solution Number 97

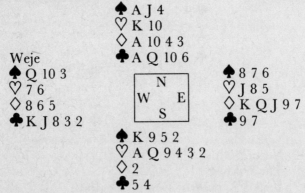

♠ A J 4
♡ K 10
◊ A 10 4 3
♣ A Q 10 6

Weje
♠ Q 10 3
♡ 7 6
◊ 8 6 5
♣ K J 8 3 2

♠ 8 7 6
♡ J 8 5
◊ K Q J 9 7
♣ 9 7

♠ K 9 5 2
♡ A Q 9 4 3 2
◊ 2
♣ 5 4

Open Pairs Championships, Copenhagen, 1960.
    Contract: 4♡. Lead ◊8.
    Having cashed the ◊A and three rounds of trumps declarer then played the ♠2 to dummy's jack, and drew the ♠A. Christian Weje was thus given the opportunity of trying out the good

old text-book trick of dropping the ♠Q. This gave him a trick with the ♠10 which declarer naturally enough tried to pick up from East, and only two overtricks were made instead of three.

At another table Helge Kruse-Hansen made the same defence, but the declarer, Niels Müller, had also read the text-book, and anyway, he was also too well aware of Kruse-Hansen's craftiness (or perhaps he had too innocent an expression), so Müller went up with the king and took all the tricks. It may be recalled that a Norwegian, Mrs Pihl, played similarly in a duplicate in 1968.

Solution Number 98

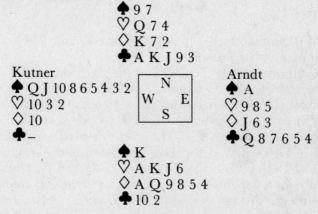

European Ladies' Championship, Estoril, 1970. Switzerland-Holland.

Contract: 6◇. Lead ♠2.

Mrs Arndt, winning with the ♠A, understood correctly the very low spade as being Lavinthal's suit-preference signal; she switched to the ♠8 which Mrs Y. Kutner ruffed. She led the ♠Q. To get more than the one undertrick was, however, impossible but in the circumstances satisfactory.

This defence was in no way exceptional, and would be made as a matter of course by all experienced players. My real reason, however, for including this particular deal is to show that it has quite another interest. With no stopper in spades North-South would have an ice-cold small slam in no trumps!

141

Solution Number 99

```
                    ♠ —
                    ♡ A 10 5 3 2
                    ◊ K J 6 4
                    ♣ K J 7 6
                                        Poubeau
♠ K J 8 6 5 4              N           ♠ 9 3
♡ —                  W          E      ♡ K Q J 8 7 4
◊ 5 2                      S           ◊ Q 10 9
♣ A 10 5 3 2                          ♣ 9 8
                    ♠ A Q 10 7 2
                    ♡ 9 6
                    ◊ A 8 7 3
                    ♣ Q 4
```

World Championships, Open Pairs, Stockholm, 1970.
   Contract: 3 No Trumps. Lead ♣3.
   Declarer ducked to the queen in the closed hand and continued with the ♣4 to dummy's jack so as to play the ♡2.
Dominique Poubeau won with the ♡J and, as you will have
surely guessed, then switched to the ♣9 which West won with
the ♣J over declarer's ♣10. However, the precision and fine
detail of East's play will not be seen until later. West then
switched to the ◊5, covered by the ◊J, Q and A. Declarer
returned the ◊8 to dummy's king and played the ◊4. Poubeau
won with the ◊10 and played the ♣3. This time declarer went
up with the ♣A, played the ◊3 (having unblocked the ◊7
previously) to dummy's ◊6 and led a low heart from dummy.
He felt quite sure that he had endplayed Poubeau who, he
thought, would be able only to return hearts into dummy's
tenace. His vision of victory was short-lived, for the very good
reason that Poubeau ducked with the ♡7! Declarer had, thus,
to win the trick with the ♡9 and, inevitably, give West the last
three tricks with the ♣K-8 and the ♣A.

142

Deal Number 100

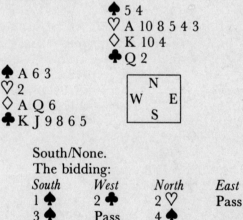

♠ Q 10 9 3
♡ A 3
◇ J 7 6 5 4 2
♣ K

♠ J 8 4
♡ K J 6
◇ 10 9
♣ A J 9 4 2

```
      N
  W       E
      S
```

South/None.
The bidding:

South	North
1 ♠	4 ♠
4 NT	5 ◇
6 ♠	

West leads the ♣A drawing the ♣K, 3 and 7. What now?

Deal Number 101

♠ 5 4
♡ A 10 8 5 4 3
◇ K 10 4
♣ Q 2

♠ A 6 3
♡ 2
◇ A Q 6
♣ K J 9 8 6 5

```
      N
  W       E
      S
```

South/None.
The bidding:

South	West	North	East
1 ♠	2 ♣	2 ♡	Pass
3 ♣	Pass	4 ♠	

West leads the ♡2. Low hearts from dummy and East.
Declarer wins with the ♡9 and plays the ♠K. How does West
plan the defence?

143

Deal Number 102

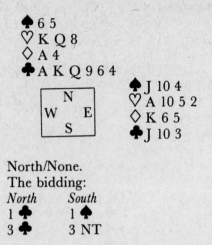

♠ 6 5
♡ K Q 8
♢ A 4
♣ A K Q 9 6 4

♠ J 10 4
♡ A 10 5 2
♢ K 6 5
♣ J 10 3

North/None.
The bidding:

North	South
1 ♣	1 ♠
3 ♣	3 NT

West leads the ♢J. Dummy ducks. East wins with the ♢K and switches to spades. He is allowed to hold both the ♠J and 10 What now?

Solution Number 100

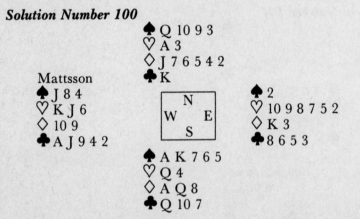

♠ Q 10 9 3
♡ A 3
♢ J 7 6 5 4 2
♣ K

Mattsson
♠ J 8 4
♡ K J 6
♢ 10 9
♣ A J 9 4 2

♠ 2
♡ 10 9 8 7 5 2
♢ K 3
♣ 8 6 5 3

♠ A K 7 6 5
♡ Q 4
♢ A Q 8
♣ Q 10 7

Olympiad at Miami, June 1972. 18th round: Germany-South Africa.

Contract: 6♠. Lead ♣A.

The Swedish-born player in the German team, Goeran Mattsson, switched to the ♢9, this lead making declarer believe

144

that East held ◇K-10-3. So, declarer covered with dummy's ◇J and took East's king with the ace. But when, later in the play, he took a diamond finesse through East, Mattsson took the setting trick with the ◇10.

Solution Number 101

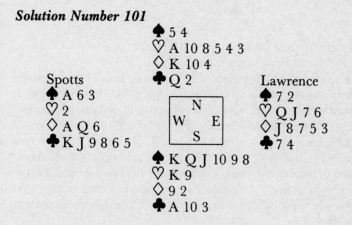

Duplicate at San Francisco, 1968.
  Contract: 4♠. Lead ♡2.

  Declarer won the trick with the ♡9 and followed with the ♠K. To break the trump connexion to the closed hand Robert L. Spotts ducked the first spade, but he took the next spade with the ace. The question was now to get East on lead, and in an attempt to do this he led the ◇Q. It was evident that South could not afford to duck, and so he covered with the ◇K. He breathed a sigh of relief when it held. Then to create an entry without opening the club suit he continued with the ◇4. Michael Lawrence was only too well aware of what was going on, so he went up with the ◇J to then play a heart for Spotts to ruff. Exiting with the ◇A he could, with a little patience, look forward to the undertrick in clubs.

```
                         ♠ 6 5
                         ♡ K Q 8
                         ◇ A 4
                         ♣ A K Q 9 6 4   Scheuer
        ♠ K Q 9 2        ┌─────────┐     ♠ J 10 4
        ♡ J 3            │    N    │     ♡ A 10 5 2
        ◇ J 10 9 8 7     │ W     E │     ◇ K 6 5
        ♣ 5 2            │    S    │     ♣ J 10 3
                         └─────────┘
                         ♠ A 8 7 3
                         ♡ 9 7 6 4
                         ◇ Q 3 2
                         ♣ 8 7
```

Duplicate at Boston, in the late thirties.

Contract: 3 No Trumps. Lead ◇J.

With open cards it is clear that the contract would be cold if declarer should go up with dummy's ace. He ducked instead, Jerome Scheuer won with the ◇K and switched to spades. Again declarer ducked both the ♠J and the ♠10, so that West's eventual long spade would be blocked. However Scheuer was happy with the two spade tricks—he saw that should West happen to have the ♡J the South hand could be blocked, and so he switched to the ♡2. Scheuer's wish was granted and he won the last two tricks with his heart tenace. Thus the contract went down one.

146

Deal Number 103

♠ 5 4 2
♡ K 7 5 2
♢ J 9 6 4
♣ K 5

♠ K
♡ A J 9 3
♢ A K 8 7 3
♣ Q 10 6

West/East–West.
The bidding:

West	North	East	South
1 ♢	Pass	1 NT	2 ♠
Pass	Pass	Double	

West leads the ♠K, holding the trick. What does West lead now?

Deal Number 104

♠ A 9 7 2
♡ –
♢ 9 8 7 4
♣ K Q 8 3 2

♠ K J 10 5
♡ J 10 5
♢ K 5
♣ J 7 6 5

North/North–South.
The bidding:

North	South
Pass	1 ♢
1 ♠	2 ♡
3 ♣	3 ♡
4 ♢	4 ♡

West leads the ♣3. Dummy ducks. East wins with the ♠K and returns the ♠5 to declarer's queen. After three rounds of trumps declarer plays the ♣9. West goes up with the ♣A and exits with a trump. Declarer cashes the ♢A and continues with the ♢2. How does East plan the defence?

147

Deal Number 105

♠ Q
♡ K Q 9 8 2
◇ A 10 4 2
♣ A 8 4

♠ A J 9 8 5 4 2
♡ –
◇ K J
♣ Q J 7 2

N
W E
S

West/None.
Partscores: North–South 60, East–West 90.
The bidding:

West	North	East	South
2 ♠	Double	3 ♡	Pass
3 ♠	Pass	Pass	4 ◇
4 ♠	5 ◇	Pass	Pass
Double			

West leads the ♠A and continues with the ♠9. Dummy ruffs with the ◇2, but East overruffs with the ◇3, cashes the ♡A and continues with the ♡10, South following. How does West plan the defence from here?

Solution Number 103

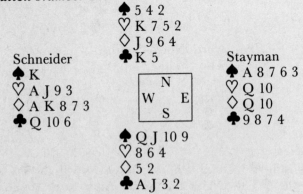

♠ 5 4 2
♡ K 7 5 2
◇ J 9 6 4
♣ K 5

Schneider
♠ K
♡ A J 9 3
◇ A K 8 7 3
♣ Q 10 6

Stayman
♠ A 8 7 6 3
♡ Q 10
◇ Q 10
♣ 9 8 7 4

N
W E
S

♠ Q J 10 9
♡ 8 6 4
◇ 5 2
♣ A J 3 2

Rubber Bridge at Monte Carlo, 1960.
Contract: 2 ♠ doubled. Lead ♠K.

It was fortunate that Sam Stayman of the United States had bid 1 No Trump and not 1 ♠. The Austrian Karl Schneider evidently knew the maxim 'Lead trumps when your partner doubles'; this was laid down in the twenties by the Danish bridge theorist and statistician Alfred Müller.

After cashing the ♠K Schneider switched to the ◇7. Stayman won with the ◇10, drew the ♠A and the ◇Q, and then a low trump. The result was that declarer won only two tricks in each of the black suits, for the very good reason that Schneider when declarer led a heart from the closed hand went up with the ace; he then played the ◇K so that Stayman could discard his second heart.

Solution Number 104

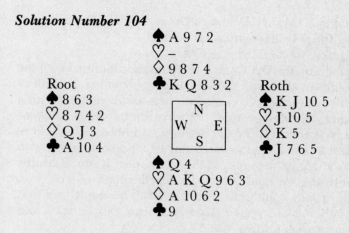

```
                    ♠ A 9 7 2
                    ♡ –
                    ◇ 9 8 7 4
                    ♣ K Q 8 3 2
  Root                                    Roth
  ♠ 8 6 3                                 ♠ K J 10 5
  ♡ 8 7 4 2          N                    ♡ J 10 5
  ◇ Q J 3        W       E                ◇ K 5
  ♣ A 10 4           S                    ♣ J 7 6 5
                    ♠ Q 4
                    ♡ A K Q 9 6 3
                    ◇ A 10 6 2
                    ♣ 9
```

Olympiad at Deauville, 1968. USA-Venezuela.

Contract: 4♡. Lead ♠3.

The opening lead was a killer. Alvin Roth won the trick with the ♠K and returned the ♠5 to declarer's queen. From then on dummy was completely blocked. Following three rounds of trumps declarer led the ♣9. William Root went up with the ace and exited with his last trump. Declarer won and drew the ◇A. Roth now unblocked the ◇K. From then on two diamond tricks had to be lost, with the result one down.

At the other table the opening lead was a diamond, and, therefore, declarer could play clubs while the ♠A was an entry to dummy.

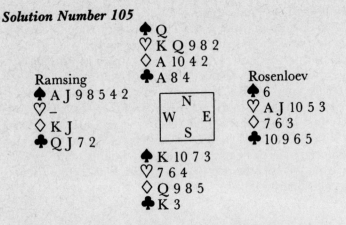

♠ Q
♡ K Q 9 8 2
◇ A 10 4 2
♣ A 8 4

Ramsing
♠ A J 9 8 5 4 2
♡ –
◇ K J
♣ Q J 7 2

```
      N
   W     E
      S
```

Rosenloev
♠ 6
♡ A J 10 5 3
◇ 7 6 3
♣ 10 9 6 5

♠ K 10 7 3
♡ 7 6 4
◇ Q 9 8 5
♣ K 3

International Match Denmark-Great Britain, Copenhagen, 1932. Rubber Bridge with total points.

Contract: 5◇ doubled. Lead ♠A.

Having won the ♠A Carl C. U. Ramsing continued with the ♠9. Dummy ruffed with the ◇2. However Knud H. Rosenloev overruffed with the ◇3, cashed the ♡A and continued with a low heart. Ramsing promptly ruffed with the ◇K(!) and continued in spades. Of course, declarer had been led to believe that East was holding the remaining trumps, so he ruffed with dummy's ◇A; he then played the ◇10 and let it run. Ramsing won with the ◇J, and then led a fourth round of spades so that Rosenloev could ruff with his ◇7. The result was that Ramsing's ingenuity gave East-West two extra tricks, and the contract went down four.

Exactly the same defence was made by Benito Garozzo 32 years later against Spain in the Olympiad in New York, as well as by Bennie Ignatz in 1967 in an American duplicate; and Edward Mayer some years ago in England.

Deal Number 106

```
                    ♠ K Q 10 3 2
                    ♡ J 7 3
                    ◇ A 9
                    ♣ A 10 9
♠ 9
♡ 6 2                    ┌───────┐
◇ K J 10 6 3 2          │   N   │
♣ K 7 4 3              │ W   E │
                        │   S   │
                        └───────┘
```

South/None.
The bidding:

South	West	North	East
1 ♡	2 ◇	2 ♠	Pass
3 ♡	Pass	4 ♡	

West leads the ♠9. East wins with the ace and returns the ♠5, ruffed by West. What does West lead now?

Deal Number 107

```
                    ♠ A K J 10
                    ♡ Q J
                    ◇ A K Q 8
                    ♣ 6 4 2
                                    ♠ 7 6 2
                    ┌───────┐       ♡ 5
                    │   N   │       ◇ J 9 7 4 3
                    │ W   E │       ♣ 10 8 7 3
                    │   S   │
                    └───────┘
```

West/North–South.
The bidding:

West	North	East	South
1 ♡	Double	Pass	1 ♠
2 ♡	2 ♠	Pass	3 ♠
Pass	4 ♠		

West leads the ♡K and continues with the ♡A. What card does East play?

151

Deal Number 108

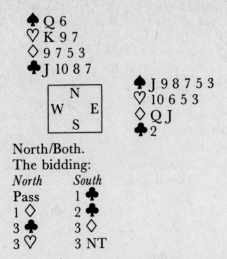

♠ Q 6
♡ K 9 7
◇ 9 7 5 3
♣ J 10 8 7

♠ J 9 8 7 5 3
♡ 10 6 5 3
◇ Q J
♣ 2

North/Both.
The bidding:

North	South
Pass	1 ♣
1 ◇	2 ♣
3 ♣	3 ◇
3 ♡	3 NT

West leads the ♡A and continues with the ♡Q to dummy's king, declarer following with the ♡J. Declarer runs five club tricks, West discarding the ♡4 and the ♠4, dummy the ◇3 and East four low spades. Then declarer lays down the ◇A followed by the ◇2. West follows with the ◇10 and East wins with the ◇Q. What now?

Solution Number 106

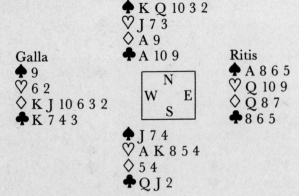

♠ K Q 10 3 2
♡ J 7 3
◇ A 9
♣ A 10 9

Galla
♠ 9
♡ 6 2
◇ K J 10 6 3 2
♣ K 7 4 3

Ritis
♠ A 8 6 5
♡ Q 10 9
◇ Q 8 7
♣ 8 6 5

♠ J 7 4
♡ A K 8 5 4
◇ 5 4
♣ Q J 2

World Championships in Stockholm, 1970. Italy-Norway.
Contract: 4♡. Lead ♠9.

Bruno De Ritis won with the ♠A and returned ♠5. Vittorio La Galla ruffed and switched to the ♣7. To declarer the ♠5 looked very much like a suit-preference signal to the ♣K. As he saw it he dared not finesse and thus risk another spade ruff. Instead he went up with the ♣A, and so drew trumps. His hope was for the doubleton ♡Q but he was unlucky, and the contract went down one.

You will perhaps remember that this was the year when neither Italy's 'blue' team played nor, indeed, did its 'light blues', but nevertheless this which I suppose could be described as a 'C-team', played remarkably well.

Solution Number 107

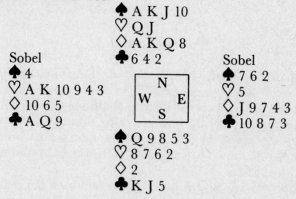

Sobel
♠ A K J 10
♡ Q J
♢ A K Q 8
♣ 6 4 2

Sobel
♠ 4
♡ A K 10 9 4 3
♢ 10 6 5
♣ A Q 9

Sobel
♠ 7 6 2
♡ 5
♢ J 9 7 4 3
♣ 10 8 7 3

♠ Q 9 8 5 3
♡ 8 7 6 2
♢ 2
♣ K J 5

This was a Mixed Pairs played in the United States many years ago when Helen Smith was still Helen Sobel.

Contract: 4♠. Lead ♡K.

Alexander M. Sobel continued with the ♡A, and Helen Sobel could see clearly that should the defenders win two more tricks then it could only be in clubs, and also that it must be a matter of urgency. So she ruffed the second heart and switched to clubs. After cashing his two club tricks Al Sobel, with good reason, said: 'You ruffed my ace—thank you partner.'

I wonder what would have been the result in the old frontier days when men were shot for ruffing their partner's aces.

At the Summer National at Los Angeles in 1963 two women lived to survive ruffing their partners' aces, Stella Rebner in the Mixed-Teams and Terry Michaels in a Charity Match. In the matches mentioned it is quite evident that an extra trick went to the defenders.

Solution Number 108

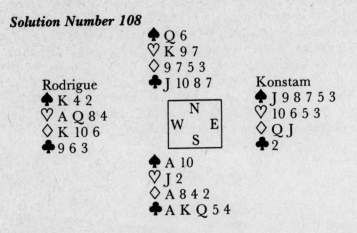

Rodrigue
♠ K 4 2
♡ A Q 8 4
◇ K 10 6
♣ 9 6 3

♠ Q 6
♡ K 9 7
◇ 9 7 5 3
♣ J 10 8 7

Konstam
♠ J 9 8 7 5 3
♡ 10 6 5 3
◇ Q J
♣ 2

♠ A 10
♡ J 2
◇ A 8 4 2
♣ A K Q 5 4

World Championships in New York, 1962. Great Britain-Italy. Contract: 3 No Trumps. Lead ♡A.

Suspicious of the heart bid Claude Rodrigue led the ♡A, to continue with the ♡Q to dummy's king. On five rounds of clubs West discarded the ♡4 and the ♠4, dummy the ◇3 and East four low spades. Then declarer cashed the ◇A and continued with the ◇2.

Winning with the ◇Q Kenneth Konstam took the reasonable view that declarer would be unlikely to be holding another king, for if he had he would doubtless have taken his nine tricks. Instead, therefore, of cashing his heart tricks Konstam switched to the ♠9! Declarer decided not to let a chance like this be lost to make the contract, so he ducked with the ♠10. Rodrigue won with the ♠K and cashed the ◇K. Konstam threw his last spade and won the last two tricks in hearts. Down two.

Deal Number 109

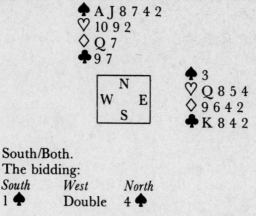

♠ A J 8 7 4 2
♡ 10 9 2
♢ Q 7
♣ 9 7

♠ 3
♡ Q 8 5 4
♢ 9 6 4 2
♣ K 8 4 2

South/Both.
The bidding:

South	West	North
1 ♠	Double	4 ♠

West leads the ♡K, then the ♡A. Declarer ruffs with the ♠6 and plays the ♠9 to dummy's ace to lead the ♣7 from dummy. What card does East play?

Deal Number 110

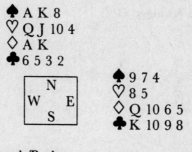

♠ A K 8
♡ Q J 10 4
♢ A K
♣ 6 5 3 2

♠ 9 7 4
♡ 8 5
♢ Q 10 6 5
♣ K 10 9 8

South/Both.
The bidding:

South	North
1 ♡	4 NT
5 ♡	5 NT
6 ♢	6 ♡

West leads the ♣Q. Declarer wins and draws two rounds of trumps, thereafter a spade to dummy to ruff the ♣8. After cashing the two high diamonds he plays the ♣2 from dummy. With what card does East follow and why?

Deal Number 111

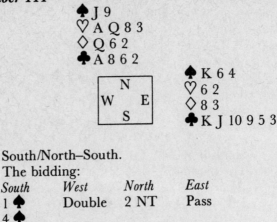

♠ J 9
♡ A Q 8 3
♢ Q 6 2
♣ A 8 6 2

♠ K 6 4
♡ 6 2
♢ 8 3
♣ K J 10 9 5 3

South/North–South.
The bidding:

South	West	North	East
1 ♠	Double	2 NT	Pass
4 ♠			

West leads the ♡J. Declarer wins with dummy's ace and plays the ♠9. How does East plan the defence?

Solution Number 109

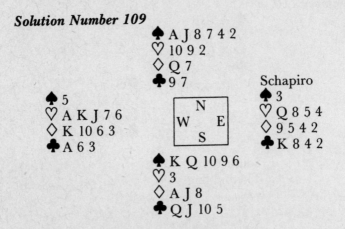

♠ A J 8 7 4 2
♡ 10 9 2
♢ Q 7
♣ 9 7

Schapiro

♠ 5
♡ A K J 7 6
♢ K 10 6 3
♣ A 6 3

♠ 3
♡ Q 8 5 4
♢ 9 5 4 2
♣ K 8 4 2

♠ K Q 10 9 6
♡ 3
♢ A J 8
♣ Q J 10 5

Rubber Bridge in London, 1969.
Contract: 4♠. Lead ♡K, then ♡A.

South ruffed the second heart and played the ♠9 to the ace so that he could lead the ♣7 from dummy.

Whist players are aware that one of the golden rules in their game is 'Second hand low'. This is also valid in bridge,

156

although there can be certain exceptions to it. Boris Schapiro is said to have a special flair for doing the 'wrong thing' at the right time, and in this particular case he had in mind the actual distribution where West would eventually win with the ♣A, be unable to switch to diamonds, and thus give declarer time to set up clubs for a diamond discard from dummy. So Schapiro went up with the ♣K in the second hand, held the trick, and switched to a diamond, with the result that West's ♢K was set up for the undertrick.

Solution Number 110

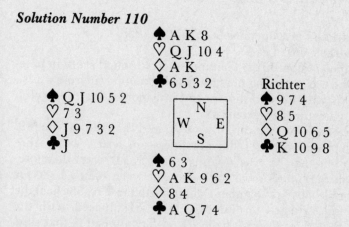

```
              ♠ A K 8
              ♡ Q J 10 4
              ◇ A K
              ♣ 6 5 3 2
                                    Richter
  ♠ Q J 10 5 2                      ♠ 9 7 4
  ♡ 7 3            N                ♡ 8 5
  ◇ J 9 7 3 2    W   E              ◇ Q 10 6 5
  ♣ J              S                ♣ K 10 9 8
              ♠ 6 3
              ♡ A K 9 6 2
              ◇ 8 4
              ♣ A Q 7 4
```

Duplicate in Copenhagen, 1960.
    Contract: 6♡. Lead ♠Q.
After drawing the trumps in two rounds and eliminating spades and diamonds declarer played the ♣2 from dummy. His aim, if he could manage it, was to duck the club to West, and within this distribution, the plan was perfectly feasible as West must give declarer a ruff and discard so that he could throw a club and eventually finesse the ♣K.

However, Einar Richter from past experience, was only too well aware of South's plan and ruined it by going up with the ♣K. The result was that declarer had to lose two club tricks to Richter, and went one down.

This, as can be seen, was a variation of the 'Crocodile Coup'.

♠ J 9
♡ A Q 8 3
◊ Q 6 2
♣ A 8 6 2

Gemmer
♠ K 6 4
♡ 6 2
◊ 8 3
♣ K J 10 9 5 3

♠ A 7
♡ J 10 9 7
◊ K 10 9 4
♣ Q 7 4

♠ Q 10 8 5 3 2
♡ K 5 4
◊ A J 7 5
♣ —

Mixed-Pairs in Copenhagen, October 1958.
  Contract: 4♠. Lead ♡J.
  In the auction Birthe Gemmer showed sound sense in passing. She was not going to scare North-South away from a 3 No Trumps contract, and she was certainly not interested in a club lead against a spade contract.
  Declarer won with dummy's ♡A, and then played the ♠9. The fact that declarer did not finesse in hearts was a sure indication that he was holding the ♡K. It was, therefore, possible that the ♠A was somewhere between West's assets for the double. So Mrs Gemmer went up with the ♠K. She held the trick and switched to diamonds. Declarer ducked, with the result that West won with the ◊K and continued in that suit. When he took the next trump round with the ♠A he played a third diamond for his partner to ruff, so the contract was down one.

Deal Number 112

```
                    ♠ 9 5 2
                    ♡ K J 7
                    ◇ K 8 4 2
                    ♣ 8 6 3
♠ Q J 10              ┌─────────┐
♡ 8 3 2               │    N    │
◇ J 7 5               │ W     E │
♣ A J 10 2            │    S    │
                      └─────────┘
```

South/Both.
The bidding:

South	North
1 ♡	2 ♡
4 ♡	

West leads the ♠Q. East follows with the ♠8 and declarer wins with the ♠A. He plays the ◇6 to dummy's king to play the ♣3 to the king in the closed hand. How does West plan the defence?

Deal Number 113

```
                    ♠ 10 2
                    ♡ Q 9 2
                    ◇ Q 9 5 2
                    ♣ J 10 9 4
♠ A 6                 ┌─────────┐
♡ A J 10 8 5          │    N    │
◇ 7 4                 │ W     E │
♣ A K 8 6             │    S    │
                      └─────────┘
```

West/Both.
The bidding:

West	North	East	South
1 ♡	Pass	2 ♡	2 ♠
3 ♡	Pass	Pass	3 ♠
4 ♡	Pass	Pass	4 ♠
Double			

West leads the ♣K, East following with the ♣2 and South with the ♣Q. What now?

159

Deal Number 114

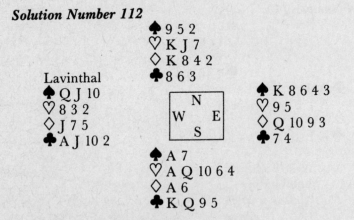

```
                    ♠ J
                    ♡ 8 7 5 3 2
                    ◇ A K J 5
                    ♣ 9 7 4
♠ 9 7 3
♡ A 6 4              ┌─────────┐
◇ 9 8 7 4 3         │    N    │
♣ A Q               │ W     E │
                    │    S    │
                    └─────────┘
```

West/East–West.
The bidding:

West	North	East	South
Pass	Pass	1 ♣	2 ♠
Double			

West cashes the ♣A and Q, East following with the ♣6 and 8 and South with the ♣2 and 10. What now?

Solution Number 112

```
                    ♠ 9 5 2
                    ♡ K J 7
                    ◇ K 8 4 2
Lavinthal           ♣ 8 6 3
♠ Q J 10                                  ♠ K 8 6 4 3
♡ 8 3 2             ┌─────────┐          ♡ 9 5
◇ J 7 5             │    N    │          ◇ Q 10 9 3
♣ A J 10 2          │ W     E │          ♣ 7 4
                    │    S    │
                    └─────────┘
                    ♠ A 7
                    ♡ A Q 10 6 4
                    ◇ A 6
                    ♣ K Q 9 5
```

Duplicate in USA, 1970.
Contract: 4♡. Lead ♠Q.
Declarer won with the ♠A and played the ◇6 to dummy's king to lead the ♣3 to the king in the closed hand. Sylvia Lavinthal dropped the ♣2. Possibly declarer had no experience of feminine wiles, at least in bridge, so he cashed three

160

rounds of trumps ending in dummy to play another club to the queen. The feline Sylvia Lavinthal won with aplomb and cashed two more clubs in addition to the ♠J. The contract went down one.

Should West have won the first club declarer could easily have made the contract by cashing the ♣Q, losing a club, and then ruffing the fourth club with one of dummy's honours.

Solution Number 113

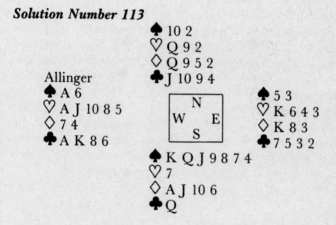

```
                    ♠ 10 2
                    ♡ Q 9 2
                    ◇ Q 9 5 2
                    ♣ J 10 9 4
      Allinger
      ♠ A 6                           ♠ 5 3
      ♡ A J 10 8 5       N           ♡ K 6 4 3
      ◇ 7 4          W       E       ◇ K 8 3
      ♣ A K 8 6          S           ♣ 7 5 3 2
                    ♠ K Q J 9 8 7 4
                    ♡ 7
                    ◇ A J 10 6
                    ♣ Q
```

Duplicate in USA, 1967.

Contract: 4♠ doubled. Lead ♣K.

Paul Allinger was fast beginning to regret his double, for his dread was that declarer could win unless East could get a diamond trick. If, however, East held the ◇K it could be finessed, provided that declarer was allowed to get into dummy on the ♠10. Bravely Allinger led the ♠6, catching declarer dreaming when he followed with the ♠2 from dummy. Was his hope that East would win with the ace, or was he not using his intelligence? At any rate the chance was lost to get into dummy, and a trick was lost in each of the four suits.

Solution Number 114

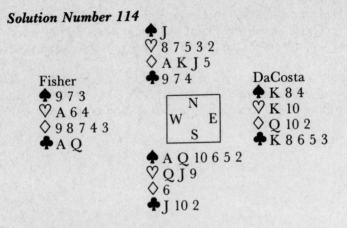

```
                    ♠ J
                    ♡ 8 7 5 3 2
                    ◇ A K J 5
                    ♣ 9 7 4
Fisher                              DaCosta
♠ 9 7 3             N               ♠ K 8 4
♡ A 6 4        W         E          ♡ K 10
◇ 9 8 7 4 3        S               ◇ Q 10 2
♣ A Q                               ♣ K 8 6 5 3
                    ♠ A Q 10 6 5 2
                    ♡ Q J 9
                    ◇ 6
                    ♣ J 10 2
```

Mixed-Teams in Canada, 1968.

Contract: 2♠ doubled. Lead ♣A.

Don DaCosta followed with the ♣6, but when Cecille Fisher continued with the ♣Q he dropped the ♣8. She understood this to be a suit-preference signal and so she switched to the ♡4. DaCosta won with the ♡K. cashed the ♣K, then switched back to hearts and ruffed a third round in that suit. DaCosta now played a club to the triple void and so made sure of another trump trick for the defenders. If declarer should win in the closed hand with the ♠10 West's ♠9 would sooner or later be promoted, and if he should win in dummy he would be unable to finesse in trumps. So the contract went down two.

Deal Number 115

```
                  ♠ K 10 5
                  ♡ Q 10 9 7 5 4
                  ◇ –
                  ♣ A J 3 2
♠ Q 9 8 7 3 2            ┌─────────┐
♡ 3                     │    N    │
◇ Q 4                   │ W     E │
♣ K Q 10 9              │    S    │
                        └─────────┘
```

North/Both.
The bidding:

North	East	South	West
1 ♡	Pass	2 ◇	2 ♠
Pass	Pass	3 NT	

West leads the ♣K. Declarer wins with dummy's ace to play the ♡4. East wins the trick with the ♡J and exits with his last club. West wins with the queen and plays a third round of clubs to dummy's ♣J. A low heart is taken with the king by East who switches to a diamond. Declarer wins with the ◇K and plays the ♠6. Now it is up to West?

Deal Number 116

```
                  ♠ A Q 6 4 2
                  ♡ 5
                  ◇ 8 7 2
                  ♣ A Q 10 7
                        ┌─────────┐   ♠ J 8 5
                        │    N    │   ♡ A K J 9 7 4 3
                        │ W     E │   ◇ Q
                        │    S    │   ♣ K J
                        └─────────┘
```

East/North–South.
The bidding:

East	South	West	North
1 ♡	Pass	Pass	Double
2 ♡	2 ♠	3 ◇	3 ♠
Pass	Pass	4 ♡	Pass
Pass	Double	Pass	4 ♠
Double			

163

West leads the ♡2. East wins with the ♡K and switches to the ◊Q. Declarer wins with the ace, ruffs a heart, draws three rounds of trumps and plays a low club to the ace? What is East's plan?

Deal Number 117

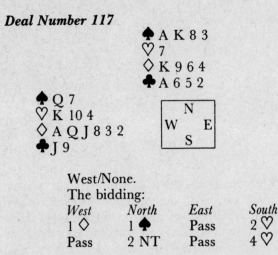

```
              ♠ A K 8 3
              ♡ 7
              ◊ K 9 6 4
              ♣ A 6 5 2
♠ Q 7                        N
♡ K 10 4                  W     E
◊ A Q J 8 3 2                S
♣ J 9
```

West/None.
The bidding:

West	North	East	South
1 ◊	1 ♠	Pass	2 ♡
Pass	2 NT	Pass	4 ♡

West leads the ◊A, then the ◊Q, covered by dummy's king and ruffed by East with the ♡5. East switches to a low club which declarer lets run to dummy's ace in order to play the ♡7 and finesse with the ♡Q, East following with the ♡2. How does West continue the defence?

Solution Number 115

```
                    ♠ K 10 5
                    ♡ Q 10 9 7 5 4
                    ◊ −
Pavlicek            ♣ A J 3 2
♠ Q 9 8 7 3 2                          ♠ 4
♡ 3                      N             ♡ A K J 6
◊ Q 4                 W     E          ◊ 10 9 8 7 3 2
♣ K Q 10 9              S              ♣ 5 4
                    ♠ A J 6
                    ♡ 8 2
                    ◊ A K J 6 5
                    ♣ 8 7 6
```

164

Knock-out Championships in Washington, July 1973.

Contract: 3 No Trumps. Lead ♣K.

Declarer won with dummy's ace. He then led the ♡4 which was taken with the jack by East, who returned his last club. Richard Pavlicek went up with the queen and then led a third club. Dummy won and continued in hearts. East, winning with the king, switched to a diamond. Declarer won with the king and followed with the ♠6.

With open cards it would have been easy, but even with closed cards Pavlicek could see clearly that declarer was trying to create two spade entries in dummy, in the first place to set up the hearts and, secondly, to cash them. Pavlicek quickly put a stop to this by going up with the queen! Even if the ◇Q dropped, the contract now had to go down one.

Solution Number 116

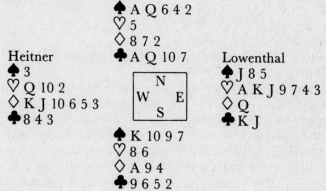

```
                    ♠ A Q 6 4 2
                    ♡ 5
                    ◇ 8 7 2
Heitner             ♣ A Q 10 7        Lowenthal
♠ 3                                   ♠ J 8 5
♡ Q 10 2          ┌─────────┐         ♡ A K J 9 7 4 3
◇ K J 10 6 5 3    │   N     │         ◇ Q
♣ 8 4 3           │ W   E   │         ♣ K J
                  │   S     │
                  └─────────┘
                    ♠ K 10 9 7
                    ♡ 8 6
                    ◇ A 9 4
                    ♣ 9 6 5 2
```

Vanderbilt Cup at Cleveland, Spring 1965.

Contract: 4♠ doubled. Lead ♡2.

John Lowenthal won with the ♡K and switched to the ◇Q. Declarer won with the ace. He then cashed three trump tricks, and continued with the ♣A as he had the feeling from the bidding that East must be holding the ♣K. His intention was to endplay East in the next trick with a low club. The reader, however, will have already guessed that John Lowenthal threw the ♣K under the ace.

If declarer should return to his hand again to finesse clubs he would have to give up the endplay, for the very good reason that his only entry would have been his last trump. Instead he led a diamond and thus allowed Peter Heitner to cash two diamonds, and then when Heitner switched to clubs declarer ducked in dummy, and the blank jack took the setting trick.

Solution Number 117

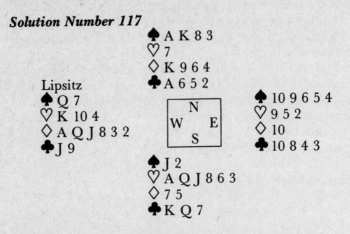

♠ A K 8 3
♡ 7
◇ K 9 6 4
♣ A 6 5 2

Lipsitz
♠ Q 7
♡ K 10 4
◇ A Q J 8 3 2
♣ J 9

♠ 10 9 6 5 4
♡ 9 5 2
◇ 10
♣ 10 8 4 3

♠ J 2
♡ A Q J 8 6 3
◇ 7 5
♣ K Q 7

Reisinger Cup at Phoenix, Arizona. November 1971.
Contract: 4♡. Lead ◇A.

Bobby Lipsitz continued with the ◇Q, and East ruffed dummy's king with the ♡5, then switched to a low club. Declarer let it run to dummy's ace so that the ♡7 could be led (East following with the ♡2) and he could finesse with the queen. This was very careless play as East with his trump echo had shown three trumps. Bobby Lipsitz won with the ♡K, and in the hope that East's third trump was high enough for an uppercut, he led the ◇2! The ♡9 was big enough to cost declarer's jack. As a result West's ♡10 became good for the setting trick.

Deal Number 118

♠ 9 7 6
♡ 10 8 7 6
◇ J 3
♣ K J 7 3

```
      N
  W       E
      S
```

♠ 10 3 2
♡ 5 4 3
◇ A 5 2
♣ A 6 5 2

West/East–West.
The bidding:

West	North	East	South
1 ♠	Pass	2 ♣	2 ♡
3 ♣	Pass	Pass	3 ◇
4 ♣	4 ♡		

West plays the three top spades. Declarer ruffs the third round and plays the ◇6 to dummy's jack. How does East plan the defence?

Deal Number 119

♠ 7 6 4
♡ K 7 2
◇ Q 8 6
♣ Q 9 8 7

```
      N
  W       E
      S
```

South/Both.
The bidding:

South	North
2 NT	3 ♣
3 ♠	4 NT
5 ♠	5 NT
6 ♣	7 NT

What card does West lead?

Deal Number 120

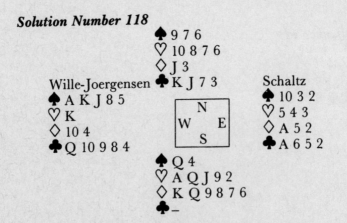

♠ J
♡ Q 9 2
♦ J 10 9 5 2
♣ A Q 4 2

♠ A K 5
♡ 7 5
♦ 8 7 4 3
♣ 10 9 8 6

N
W E
S

South/North–South.
The bidding:

South	West	North	East
1 ♠	Pass	2 ♦	2 ♡
2 ♠	Pass	2 NT	Pass
3 ♡	Pass	3 ♠	Pass
4 ♣			

West leads the ♡7. East's ♡10 forces declarer's ace. Declarer plays the ♠3. West goes up with the king and continues with the ♡5 to East's jack, and declarer ruffs the next heart with the ♠8. What is West's plan?

Solution Number 118

♠ 9 7 6
♡ 10 8 7 6
♦ J 3
♣ K J 7 3

Wille-Joergensen
♠ A K J 8 5
♡ K
♦ 10 4
♣ Q 10 9 8 4

N
W E
S

Schaltz
♠ 10 3 2
♡ 5 4 3
♦ A 5 2
♣ A 6 5 2

♠ Q 4
♡ A Q J 9 2
♦ K Q 9 8 7 6
♣ —

Mixed-Pairs in Copenhagen, 1972.
Contract: 4♡. Lead ♠K.

168

Gudrun Wille-Joergensen played three top spades. Declarer ruffed the third round and tried to enter dummy on the ♢J in an attempt for the trump finesse. Peter Schaltz, who was in a generous mood, allowed the ♢J to win the trick and thus let declarer lose the trump finesse to the blank king. Declarer had still to lose a diamond, and so went one down.

Solution Number 119

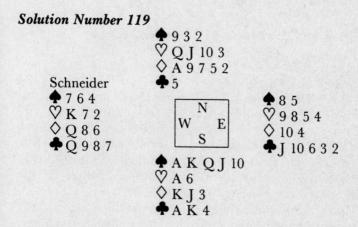

```
                    ♠ 9 3 2
                    ♡ Q J 10 3
                    ♢ A 9 7 5 2
   Schneider        ♣ 5
   ♠ 7 6 4                         ♠ 8 5
   ♡ K 7 2          ┌─────┐       ♡ 9 8 5 4
   ♢ Q 8 6        W │  N  │ E     ♢ 10 4
   ♣ Q 9 8 7        │  S  │       ♣ J 10 6 3 2
                    └─────┘
                    ♠ A K Q J 10
                    ♡ A 6
                    ♢ K J 3
                    ♣ A K 4
```

Duplicate in Paris, 1972.

Contract: 7 No Trumps. Lead ♡7.

To find the killing lead it would be necessary to imagine how declarer would have played after a neutral lead, for instance, a spade. Most of the big cards being in the closed hand, and with the apparent scarcity of entries in dummy, declarer must finesse diamonds through West to end in dummy. So Marc Schneider gave declarer an extra entry by leading the ♡7! It was quite normal, therefore, for declarer to play the ♢2 and finesse with the jack. If he had played the diamonds the other way he would have to find both the queen and the 10, but by playing as he did Marc Schneider saved the queen, and the contract went down one.

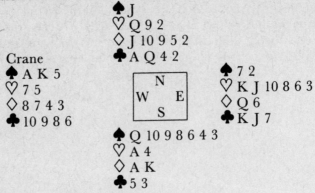

♠ J
♡ Q 9 2
◇ J 10 9 5 2
♣ A Q 4 2

Crane
♠ A K 5
♡ 7 5
◇ 8 7 4 3
♣ 10 9 8 6

♠ 7 2
♡ K J 10 8 6 3
◇ Q 6
♣ K J 7

♠ Q 10 9 8 6 4 3
♡ A 4
◇ A K
♣ 5 3

Duplicate for Lifemasters at Phoenix, Arizona. November 1971.

Contract: 4♠. Lead ♡7.

Declarer took East's ♡10 with the ace and then played the ♠3. Barry Crane, the television producer, and it may be remembered that his hobby in life is the accumulation of master points, went up with the ♠K so that he could continue with the ♡5. Declarer ruffed the third round of hearts with the ♠8. Barry Crane had no doubts—he overruffed with the ♠A and then switched to clubs. As a result declarer had to try the finesse, which went wrong, so the contract went down one.

If Crane had not overruffed declarer could have cashed the two top diamonds before continuing in trumps; as the queen dropped he could when Crane shifted to clubs go up with the ace and then throw a club on the ◇J.

Deal Number 121

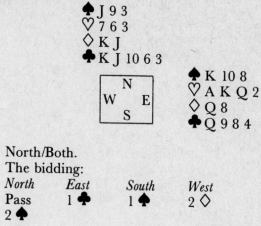

♠ J 9 3
♡ 7 6 3
◇ K J
♣ K J 10 6 3

♠ K 10 8
♡ A K Q 2
◇ Q 8
♣ Q 9 8 4

North/Both.
The bidding:

North	East	South	West
Pass	1 ♣	1 ♠	2 ◇
2 ♠			

West leads the ♠2. Dummy follows with the ♠3 and East's ♠8 forces declarer's queen. Declarer plays the ♣5 and finesses with dummy's ♣10, East winning with the queen. How does East continue?

Deal Number 122

♠ 7
♡ J 10 9
◇ A 9 5 4 3
♣ K Q 9 5

♠ A Q 9 5 3
♡ K 8 7 4
◇ 6 2
♣ 10 3

South/North–South.
The bidding:

South	West	North	East
1 ♡	3 ♠	4 ♡	4 ♠
Pass	Pass	5 ♡	

West leads the ♠K. How does East plan the defence?

Deal Number 123

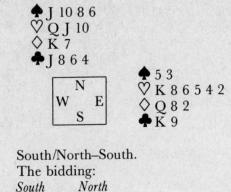

                    ♠ J 10 8 6
                    ♡ Q J 10
                    ◇ K 7
                    ♣ J 8 6 4
                                        ♠ 5 3
                                        ♡ K 8 6 5 4 2
                                        ◇ Q 8 2
                                        ♣ K 9

South/North–South.
The bidding:

South	North
1 ♠	2 ♠

West leads the ♣3 and dummy follows with the ♣4. How does
East plan the defence?

Solution Number 121

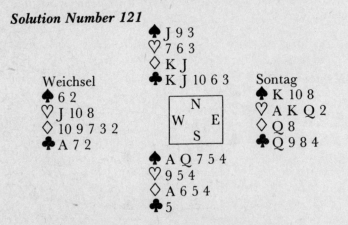

                    ♠ J 9 3
                    ♡ 7 6 3
                    ◇ K J
                    ♣ K J 10 6 3

Weichsel   Sontag
♠ 6 2   ♠ K 10 8
♡ J 10 8   ♡ A K Q 2
◇ 10 9 7 3 2   ◇ Q 8
♣ A 7 2   ♣ Q 9 8 4

                    ♠ A Q 7 5 4
                    ♡ 9 5 4
                    ◇ A 6 5 4
                    ♣ 5

Duplicate at Phoenix, Arizona, 1971.
    Contract: 2♠. Lead ♠2.
    Declarer was most disconcerted by Peter Weichsel's trump
lead. Alan Sontag covered with the ♠8, thus forcing declarer's
queen. Declarer then switched to the ♣5, finessed the jack, and
Sontag won with the ♣Q. Sontag now cashed the ♡A and the
♡Q. When Weichsel dropped the ♡J under the queen Sontag

172

played the ♡2 so that Weichsel could continue in trumps. Sontag's ♠10 cost declarer's ace.

Declarer now led the ◇4 to the jack and so gave Sontag, again, the lead on the ◇Q so that he could draw dummy's last trump before exiting with the ♡K. Declarer was still holding a diamond loser—and went down two.

Solution Number 122

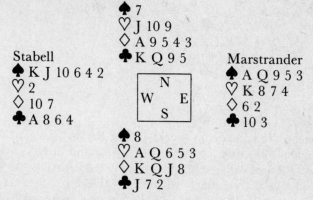

```
                    ♠ 7
                    ♡ J 10 9
                    ◇ A 9 5 4 3
                    ♣ K Q 9 5
Stabell                                  Marstrander
♠ K J 10 6 4 2          N              ♠ A Q 9 5 3
♡ 2                 W       E          ♡ K 8 7 4
◇ 10 7                  S              ◇ 6 2
♣ A 8 6 4                              ♣ 10 3
                    ♠ 8
                    ♡ A Q 6 5 3
                    ◇ K Q J 8
                    ♣ J 7 2
```

European Junior Championships at Noresund, Norway, June 1975. Norway East-West.

Contract: 5♡. Lead ♠K.

Peter Marstrander took the king over with the ace and continued with the ♠Q to a ruff and discard! A lead such as this is almost always regarded as near heresy, but in this case it was clear that it would be most embarrassing for declarer since apparently he needed no discards. If declarer were now to ruff in dummy he would be unable to draw all of East's trumps. Therefore his preference was to ruff with the ♡3, and then to lead the ♣2. But by now Leif Erik Stabell was very much on the alert—he went up with the ♣A so that he might persevere in spades. Declarer was now in the same position as before for wherever South ruffs he must lose a trump to East.

It would be of no help instead of the club switch to take the ◇K over and lead a trump from dummy, as all the trumps would be needed to draw East's. When, furthermore, he had taken his diamond tricks and had to switch to clubs Stabell would have taken the two last tricks with the ♣A and a spade.

173

Solution Number 123

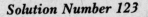

```
              ♠ J 10 8 6
              ♡ Q J 10
              ◊ K 7
Rapee         ♣ J 8 6 4         Jacoby
♠ Q 7 2                         ♠ 5 3
♡ 9            ┌─────────┐      ♡ K 8 6 5 4 2
◊ A J 10 6 4   │    N    │      ◊ Q 8 2
♣ Q 10 5 3     │  W   E  │      ♣ K 9
               │    S    │
               └─────────┘
              ♠ A K 9 4
              ♡ A 7 3
              ◊ 9 5 3
              ♣ A 7 2
```

Duplicate in USA, 1961.
   Contract: 2♠. Lead ♣3.

   Twice in the same deal Oswald Jacoby had to disregard that
well-known old rule in whist—'Third hand high'. When
dummy followed with the ♣4 Jacoby covered with only the ♣9,
which was taken by declarer with the ace. Declarer then played
the ◊3. George Rapee won with the ◊A and switched to the
♡9. Dummy was allowed to hold the trick with the ♡10, and if
declarer had now played safe he would have made three. But it
was duplicate and lightheartedly declarer tried to make four by
letting the ♠J run. Winning with the ♠Q Rapee led a club to
Jacoby's king. Jacoby played a heart for Rapee to ruff, and he
led the ♣Q. But Jacoby ruffed his trick to give him another
heart ruff, so the contract went down one.

Deal Number 124

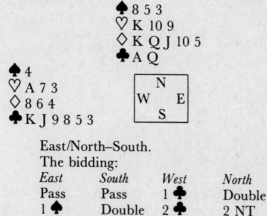

♠ Q 10 7 2
♡ 9 4
♢ J 7 4
♣ K J 5 3

♠ 9 8 6
♡ 6 2
♢ A 8 3
♣ Q 10 8 6 2

N
W E
S

South/None.
The bidding:

South	West	North	East
1 ♡	Pass	1 ♠	Pass
2 ♡	Pass	Pass	2 NT
3 ♡			

West leads the ♣6. East takes dummy's ♣J with the ace, South following with the ♣9. East shifts to the ♢2, declarer playing the king. How does West plan the defence?

Deal Number 125

♠ 8 5 3
♡ K 10 9
♢ K Q J 10 5
♣ A Q

♠ 4
♡ A 7 3
♢ 8 6 4
♣ K J 9 8 5 3

N
W E
S

East/North–South.
The bidding:

East	South	West	North
Pass	Pass	1 ♣	Double
1 ♠	Double	2 ♣	2 NT
3 ♣	4 ♡		

West leads the ♠4. East wins with the ♠A and continues with the ♠Q, covered by South with the king. How does West plan the defence?

175

♠ A K 9 5
♡ 9 6 4 2
◇ 7 2
♣ J 9 5

♠ J 10 6
♡ K 10 5
◇ A Q 8 4
♣ A 10 6

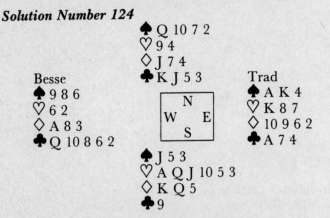

South/Both.
The bidding:
South
1 NT

West leads the ◇4 and declarer takes East's ◇9 with the jack. He plays the ♠4 to dummy's king to play the ♡2 to the ♡8 in the closed hand. How does West plan the defence?

Solution Number 124

♠ Q 10 7 2
♡ 9 4
◇ J 7 4
♣ K J 5 3

Besse
♠ 9 8 6
♡ 6 2
◇ A 8 3
♣ Q 10 8 6 2

Trad
♠ A K 4
♡ K 8 7
◇ 10 9 6 2
♣ A 7 4

♠ J 5 3
♡ A Q J 10 5 3
◇ K Q 5
♣ 9

Reykjavik, 1975. Match between the Icelandic team selected for the Nordic Championships and a visiting team from Switzerland.

Contract: 3♡. Lead ♣6.

Declarer finessed with dummy's ♣J and Tony Trad won with the ace, South followed with the ♣9. Trad switched to the ◇2 and declarer put up the king.

Jean Besse followed with the ♢3. Declarer continued with the ♢Q, but Besse ducked once more to block the dummy. Besse had to win a third diamond, so he switched to the ♠9. Tony Trad went up with the ♠K, and then played the thirteenth diamond! If declarer should now ruff with the ♡10 West would throw a spade and thus stop the later spade entry. Besse was aware from declarer's struggle to enter dummy that Trad must be holding a trump honour. It was declarer's preference to let the diamond run to dummy to ruff, and his only hope rested in East holding the ♡K doubleton—that not being the case he went down one.

Solution Number 125

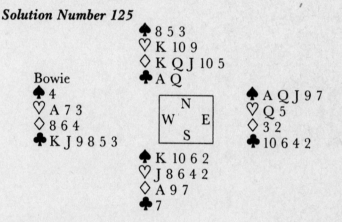

```
                      ♠ 8 5 3
                      ♡ K 10 9
                      ♢ K Q J 10 5
    Bowie             ♣ A Q
    ♠ 4                                 ♠ A Q J 9 7
    ♡ A 7 3               N             ♡ Q 5
    ♢ 8 6 4          W       E          ♢ 3 2
    ♣ K J 9 8 5 3        S              ♣ 10 6 4 2
                      ♠ K 10 6 2
                      ♡ J 8 6 4 2
                      ♢ A 9 7
                      ♣ 7
```

Duplicate in USA, in the fifties.
  Contract: 4♡. Lead ♠4.
  East won with the ♠A and continued with the ♠Q, which was covered by the ♠K by declarer.
  Clagett Bowie intended ruffing with a low trump. However, he paused to consider how East might get an entry to cash the ♠J. He felt that the only chance could be if declarer's hearts were no better than five to the jack, so that East might be holding the doubleton ♡Q. But in the event of West ruffing with a low trump, declarer at the first opportunity would enter the closed hand to play a trump to the king and thus make the ace and the queen fall together in the next trick. Bowie avoided this by throwing a club! The result was that declarer lost two

177

trump tricks; it was East who won one of them and was able to cash the ♠J so that the contract went down one.

Those of you who have read *Fairy-Tale Bridge* will almost surely remember a certain Captain Barker who was in a similar situation—his solution was even more efficient, for he ruffed the ♠K with the ♡A and then played a low trump. More recently, as has been described in *Defence at Bridge* (published in the United States as *How good is your defense?*) one, Bernasconi, has claimed to have done the same thing.

Solution Number 126

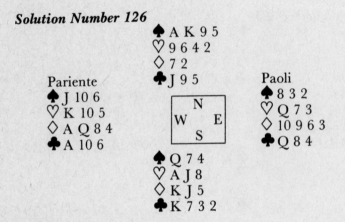

Pariente
♠ J 10 6
♡ K 10 5
◇ A Q 8 4
♣ A 10 6

(North)
♠ A K 9 5
♡ 9 6 4 2
◇ 7 2
♣ J 9 5

Paoli
♠ 8 3 2
♡ Q 7 3
◇ 10 9 6 3
♣ Q 8 4

(South)
♠ Q 7 4
♡ A J 8
◇ K J 5
♣ K 7 3 2

Paris, summer 1975.

Contract: 1 No Trump. Lead ◇4.

Declarer took East's ◇9 with the jack, played the ♠4 to dummy's king and the ♡2 to the ♡8 in the closed hand. Fanny Pariente won with the ♡10 and switched to the ♠J. Declarer won with the ♠Q, cashed the ♡A and continued with the ♡J so that dummy's fourth heart became good for the seventh trick—declarer being unaware that this had all the time been available in spades.

On the ♡A Fanny Pariente however unblocked the king. Thus Mado Paoli got the lead with the queen and could lead the ◇3. Fanny Pariente did not fall for the temptation of a deep finesse and instead she went up with the queen, drew the ace, and played the ♢8 back to Mado Paoli's ♢10. Thus declarer was forced to keep dummy's ♣J guarded, for otherwise East would have led the ♣Q. Mado Paoli then endplayed dummy with a spade, later covered the ♣J with the queen, and finished by seizing two club tricks for the defence, with the result that the contract went down one.

I should point out here that declarer could have made the contract by the immediate cashing of four spade tricks and the ♡A. With six tricks for the asking she could have exited in one of the red suits and let her opponents open up the clubs—but that, for her, is being wise after the event.

Deal Number 127

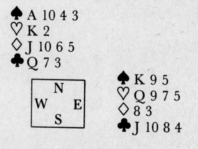

♠ A 10 4 3
♡ K 2
♢ J 10 6 5
♣ Q 7 3

♠ K 9 5
♡ Q 9 7 5
♢ 8 3
♣ J 10 8 4

North/North–South.
The bidding:

North	South
Pass	1 ♣
1 ♢	1 ♡
1 ♠	1 NT
2 NT	3 NT

West leads the ♣8 and dummy follows with the ♣3. What is East's first move?

Deal Number 128

           ♠ A 9 5 4 2
           ♡ Q 8 3 2
           ◇ A 2
           ♣ K 5

♠ K J
♡ 10 5 4
◇ K 10 7 5 4 3
♣ J 6

South/North–South.
The bidding:

South	West	North	East
Pass	Pass	1 ♠	3 ♣
3 ♡			

West leads the ♣J. East taked dummy's king, cashes the ♣Q and switches to the ◇9 which is covered with the ◇Q, K and A. Having drawn the ♡A from the closed hand and the ♡Q from dummy, declarer plays dummy's ◇2. East wins with the ◇J and plays the ♣10, declarer following with the ♣8. How does West continue the defence?

Deal Number 129

           ♠ K 9 2
           ♡ J 10 9 8 5 3
           ◇ 7 6 3
           ♣ A

                      ♠ Q 8 6 4
                      ♡ 6
                      ◇ Q J 10 8 4
                      ♣ Q 8 3

North/North–South.
The bidding:

North	East	South	West
Pass	Pass	1 NT	Pass
2 ◇ +)	Double	3 ♡	Pass
4 ♡			

+) Texas: Transfer to hearts.

West leads the ♡2. Declarer wins with the ♡A and plays the
♣4 to dummy's ace in order to lead the ◇3 to the king. West
wins with the ◇A and plays another trump. Declarer wins with
the ♡K and ruffs a club in order to lead dummy's ◇7. How
should East plan the defence?

Solution Number 127

```
                    ♠ A 10 4 3
                    ♡ K 2
                    ◇ J 10 6 5
Lawrence            ♣ Q 7 3         Goldman
♠ 8 7 2                             ♠ K 9 5
♡ 10 8 3            ┌─────────┐     ♡ Q 9 7 5
◇ K Q 9 2          │    N    │      ◇ 8 3
♣ A 6 5            │  W   E  │      ♣ J 10 8 4
                   │    S    │
                    └─────────┘
                    ♠ Q J 6
                    ♡ A J 6 4
                    ◇ A 7 4
                    ♣ K 9 2
```

World Championships at Taipei, 1971. USAces-France.
    Contract: 3 No Trumps. Lead ♠8.

When dummy ducked with the ♠3 Robert Goldman went up
with the king to exit with the ♠5 in order, as he said later, 'not
to spoil more than one suit'. Declarer won with the ♠Q, and
then played the ◇4. Michael Lawrençe won with the ◇Q and
led his last spade. Declarer let it run to the ♠J in the closed
hand, and after first cashing the ◇A, continued with the ◇7 to
West's king.

It was then that Lawrence switched to the ♡3 and declarer
was only too happy to receive that gift from the gods, a free
finesse, taking East's ♡Q with the ace. He then entered dummy
with the ◇4 to the king to cash dummy's thirteenth spade and
the good ◇J. He was now in the unenviable postion of not being
able to get back to the closed hand to the good ♡J. He tried a
club to the king, but Lawrence took the ♣K with the ace and
continued with the ♣5. Dummy, of course, won with the ♣Q,
and this was declarer's eighth, and last, trick.

Solution Number 128

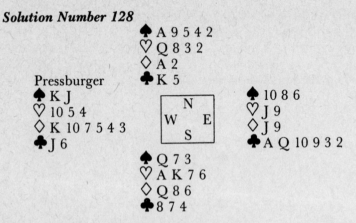

```
              ♠ A 9 5 4 2
              ♡ Q 8 3 2
              ◊ A 2
Pressburger   ♣ K 5
♠ K J                          ♠ 10 8 6
♡ 10 5 4        ┌─────────┐    ♡ J 9
◊ K 10 7 5 4 3  │    N    │    ◊ J 9
♣ J 6           │  W   E  │    ♣ A Q 10 9 3 2
                │    S    │
                └─────────┘
              ♠ Q 7 3
              ♡ A K 7 6
              ◊ Q 8 6
              ♣ 8 7 4
```

Salzburg Congress, November 1972.
    Contract: 3♡. Lead ♣J.
    Having taken the first two tricks in clubs East switched to the
◊9, covered with the ◊Q, K and A. Declarer, having drawn
two rounds of trumps with the ace and queen, led the ◊2 from
dummy. East won with the ◊J and played the ♣10. Declarer
followed with the ♣8. The German, John Pressburger, instead
of making sure of a trick for himself with the ♡10, discarded a
low diamond! Declarer ruffed in dummy and, in the hope that
East held the ♣K, led the ♣2. Pressburger took the ♣Q with
the king and then played the ♡10. The result, of course, was
that declarer had to lose two more tricks, and go down two.
    Now, had West ruffed with the ♡10 and continued with the
◊10, declarer would have achieved a complete count, thus
being able to restrict himself to one down by drawing the ♠A,
followed by a low spade to the queen—the result being that
West would have had to give him a ruff and discard.

Solution Number 129

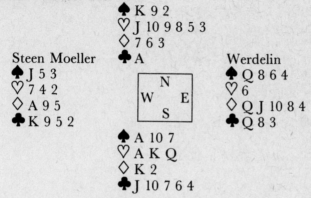

Steen Moeller ♠ K 9 2
♠ J 5 3 ♡ J 10 9 8 5 3
♡ 7 4 2 ◇ 7 6 3
◇ A 9 5 ♣ A
♣ K 9 5 2

N
W E
S

Werdelin
♠ Q 8 6 4
♡ 6
◇ Q J 10 8 4
♣ Q 8 3

♠ A 10 7
♡ A K Q
◇ K 2
♣ J 10 7 6 4

Olympiad in Monte Carlo, 1976. Denmark-Turkey.
Contract: 4♡. Lead ♡2.

Steffen Steen Moeller hit upon the good lead of a low trump.
Declarer won and played the ♣4 to dummy's ace and then led
the ◇3 covered by the ◇10, king and ace. West played another
trump. Declarer won and ruffed a club so that he could lead the
◇7 in the hope that East must win the trick. But Stig Werdelin
saw that the only chance was of West holding the ◇9 and
therefore ducked. Steen Moeller held the ◇9, and so he was able
to play a third trump, stopping declarer from ruffing a diamond
loser. Moreover, as declarer must also have to lose a spade the
contract had to go one down.

Deal Number 130

```
              ♠ 10 9 8 2
              ♡ Q 8 7
              ◇ K 6
              ♣ A Q 9 5
♠ A Q 6              ┌─────────┐
♡ A K 9 2            │    N    │
◇ J 7               │ W     E │
♣ 8 7 6 2           │    S    │
                    └─────────┘
```

South/North–South.
The bidding:

South	West	North	East
1 ◇	Double	ReDouble	Pass
1 NT	Pass	3 NT	

West leads the ♡K and switches to the ◇7. Declarer wins with the ◇10 and plays a club to dummy's ace to play the ♠10 and let it run. How does West continue the defence?

Deal Number 131

```
              ♠ 2
              ♡ 9 5
              ◇ A Q 10 8 6 3 2
              ♣ K 8 5
♠ 7 4               ┌─────────┐
♡ K 8 4 3           │    N    │
◇ K 5               │ W     E │
♣ A 7 4 3 2         │    S    │
                    └─────────┘
```

West/None.
The bidding:

West	North	East	South
Pass	Pass	3 ♠	4 ♡

184

West leads the ♠7. East wins with the king and switches to the ♡7 to reduce dummy's ruffing possibilities. Declarer covers with the ♡Q. How does West plan the defence?

Deal Number 132

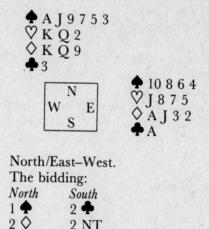

♠ A J 9 7 5 3
♡ K Q 2
♢ K Q 9
♣ 3

           ♠ 10 8 6 4
           ♡ J 8 7 5
           ♢ A J 3 2
           ♣ A

North/East–West.
The bidding:

North	South
1 ♠	2 ♣
2 ♢	2 NT
3 NT	

West leads the ♡6. Declarer takes East's ♡J with the ace and plays the ♠Q, covered by the king and ace. Dummy cashes the ♠J and continues with a low spade, East winning with the ♠8. What now?

Solution Number 130

♠ 10 9 8 2
♡ Q 8 7
♢ K 6
♣ A Q 9 5

Temime
♠ A Q 6
♡ A K 9 2
♢ J 7
♣ 8 7 6 2

           ♠ 5 4 3
           ♡ 6 5 4
           ♢ 9 8 5 4 2
           ♣ J 4

♠ K J 7
♡ J 10 3
♢ A Q 10 3
♣ K 10 3

Duplicate at the Cote d'Azur, Summer 1975.
Contract: 3 No Trumps. Lead ♡K.

Jean-Pierre Temime cashed his ♡K having the reasonable belief that declarer probably had eight tricks in the minor suits and needed only one in a major. Declarer could not know that the club suit would yield four tricks, so Temime thought of some way in which he could force him into making a mistake. He switched to the ◇7.

Declarer won with the ◇10, played the ♣3 to dummy to lead the ♣10 and let it run. The finesse was 'successful' as Temime won with the ♠A! He now exited with the ♡2 to dummy's queen. In the belief that he found the ♠Q in East declarer played for overtricks and repeated the spade finesse. However, Temime won with the ♠Q and cashed two heart tricks for one down.

Solution Number 131

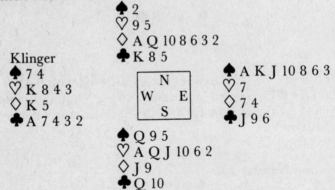

```
                    ♠ 2
                    ♡ 9 5
                    ◇ A Q 10 8 6 3 2
   Klinger          ♣ K 8 5
   ♠ 7 4                                   ♠ A K J 10 8 6 3
   ♡ K 8 4 3          N                    ♡ 7
   ◇ K 5          W       E                ◇ 7 4
   ♣ A 7 4 3 2         S                   ♣ J 9 6
                    ♠ Q 9 5
                    ♡ A Q J 10 6 2
                    ◇ J 9
                    ♣ Q 10
```

Olympiad in Monte Carlo, 1976. USA-Australia.
Contract: 4♡. Lead ♠7.

Ron Klinger led the ♠7 and East won with the king and then switched to the ♡7. As a bait for the king, declarer covered with the queen. After that all the trumps could be drawn and it would be all too easy for declarer, but Ron Klinger ducked! Declarer then ruffed a spade and played the ♣9 to the queen—not seeing that the ♣10 would have saved the day. West won with the ace and exited with a club to dummy's king. Dummy's last club was ruffed so that declarer could draw the

♡A and continue with the jack, which was taken by the king.

The really critical point had now been reached, but Klinger hit upon the killing lead—the ◇K! Declarer must win in dummy and could certainly get home on the ◇J to draw West's last trump. But if he did that then dummy was blocked and a spade would have to be lost. So instead he tried to cash two more diamonds; however, Klinger took the setting trick with the ♡8.

It will surely be remembered that this was the prize-winning hand as the best one at the Olympiad.

Solution Number 132

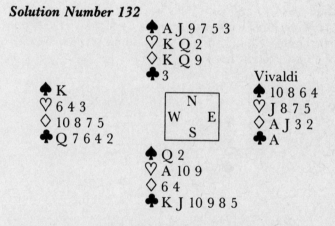

```
              ♠ A J 9 7 5 3
              ♡ K Q 2
              ◇ K Q 9
              ♣ 3
                                    Vivaldi
    ♠ K                             ♠ 10 8 6 4
    ♡ 6 4 3          N              ♡ J 8 7 5
    ◇ 10 8 7 5    W     E           ◇ A J 3 2
    ♣ Q 7 6 4 2      S              ♣ A

              ♠ Q 2
              ♡ A 10 9
              ◇ 6 4
              ♣ K J 10 9 8 5
```

Olympiad in Monte Carlo, 1976. Italy-Australia.

Contract: 3 No Trumps. Lead ♡6.

Declarer won the heart lead with the ace over East's jack, played the ♣Q, covered with the king and ace, and cashed the ♣J. Although West showed out, declarer could not do without the spades and therefore continued with a low spade for Antonio Vivaldi to win with the ♠8. Vivaldi then cashed the ♠10 and the ♣A, locking the dummy in with a heart. Finally declarer had to lose two diamonds to East, and went one down.

At the other table East had continued with a heart and thus allowed declarer to make the contract.

Deal Number 133

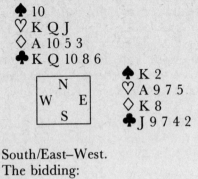

♠ 10
♡ K Q J
♢ A 10 5 3
♣ K Q 10 8 6

♠ K 2
♡ A 9 7 5
♢ K 8
♣ J 9 7 4 2

South/East–West.
The bidding:
South
4 ♠

West leads the ♢Q and continues with the ♢7 when declarer
ducks. Now declarer wins with dummy's ace, plays the ♣6 to
the ace in the closed hand and the ♡3 to dummy's jack. Now try
in East's place to find the killing defence.

Deal Number 134

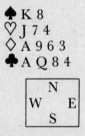

♠ K 8
♡ J 7 4
♢ A 9 6 3
♣ A Q 8 4

♠ Q 9 4
♡ 9 8 6 3
♢ K 10 7 5
♣ 9 3

North/North–South.
The bidding:

North	East	South	West
1 ♢	Pass	2 ♣	Double
ReDouble	2 ♡	3 ♣	Pass
3 ♡	Pass	3 NT	

West leads the ♣6. Dummy follows with the ♣8. How should
East plan the defence?

Deal Number 135

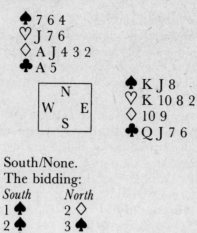

♠ 7 6 4
♡ J 7 6
◇ A J 4 3 2
♣ A 5

♠ K J 8
♡ K 10 8 2
◇ 10 9
♣ Q J 7 6

South/None.
The bidding:

South	North
1 ♠	2 ◇
2 ♠	3 ♠
4 ♠	

West leads the ♡3 and East's ♡10 costs declarer's ace. Declarer cashes the ◇K, continues with the ◇8 to dummy's jack and plays the ◇A. When East ruffs with the ♠J declarer discards the ♡4 and West drops the ◇Q. What does East lead now?

Solution Number 133

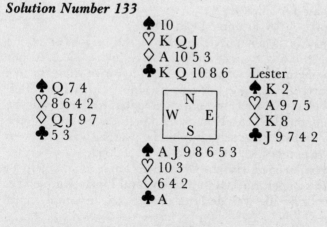

♠ 10
♡ K Q J
◇ A 10 5 3
♣ K Q 10 8 6

Lester

♠ Q 7 4
♡ 8 6 4 2
◇ Q J 9 7
♣ 5 3

♠ K 2
♡ A 9 7 5
◇ K 8
♣ J 9 7 4 2

♠ A J 9 8 6 5 3
♡ 10 3
◇ 6 4 2
♣ A

189

Australia, 1977.
    Contract: 4♠. Lead ◇Q.
    Declarer won the second diamond with dummy's ace, played the ♣6 to the ace in the closed hand and the ♡3 to dummy's jack. John Lester, the Australian International, won with the ♡A. There was now only one lead to set the contract, and he led the ♠2!

    If declarer in this situation goes up with the ace he can enter dummy in hearts and throw his diamond loser—but he will then lose two trump tricks. If he finesses by letting the ♠2 run, he only loses one trump trick, but this will be to West's ♠Q and West will be able to cash his diamond trick.

Solution Number 134

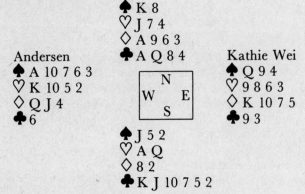

```
                    ♠ K 8
                    ♡ J 7 4
                    ◇ A 9 6 3
Andersen            ♣ A Q 8 4       Kathie Wei
♠ A 10 7 6 3                        ♠ Q 9 4
♡ K 10 5 2           ┌─────┐        ♡ 9 8 6 3
◇ Q J 4             │  N  │         ◇ K 10 7 5
♣ 6                 │W   E│         ♣ 9 3
                    │  S  │
                    └─────┘
                    ♠ J 5 2
                    ♡ A Q
                    ◇ 8 2
                    ♣ K J 10 7 5 2
```

USA Championships, 1977.
    Contract: 3 No Trumps. Lead ♠6.
    Kathe Wei is not only the wife of the originator of the Precision Bidding System and an energetic disciple of it, but she is furthermore, an expert player in her own right. In this particular game she was sitting East, her partner being Ron Andersen. (It will surely be remembered that Andersen was the winner of the 1977 McKenney competition by scoring the highest number of master points in that year; he was the first to pass 2000 points with the record score of 2009).

    Andersen opened with the ♠6 and declarer, to make sure of his spade stopper, ducked in dummy. Intuitively Kathie Wei could see from the way declarer played that he simply must have the ♠J. She was certainly not going to do his work for him and switched to the ◊5. Andersen won the trick with the ◊J, and continued with the ◊Q. Declarer had to duck this too, so as to block the long diamonds. At this state of the game Kathie Wei took the ◊Q over with the king, switching now to a heart. The inevitable happened—declarer could not win more than eight tricks.

Solution Number 135

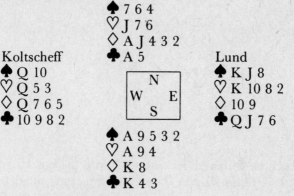

                    ♠ 7 6 4
                    ♡ J 7 6
                    ◊ A J 4 3 2
Koltscheff   ♣ A 5   Lund
♠ Q 10   ♠ K J 8
♡ Q 5 3   ┌──────────┐   ♡ K 10 8 2
◊ Q 7 6 5   │   N   │   ◊ 10 9
♣ 10 9 8 2   │ W   E │   ♣ Q J 7 6
                    │   S   │
                    └──────────┘
                    ♠ A 9 5 3 2
                    ♡ A 9 4
                    ◊ K 8
                    ♣ K 4 3

Duplicate in Copenhagen, 1978.
    Contract: 4♠. Lead ♡3.
    Alexander Koltscheff decided on the aggressive, and in fact, the only lead to set the contract—the ♡3. Peter Lund's ♡10 drew declarer's ace. Declarer cashed the ◊K, took the diamond finesse with the jack and played the ◊A. When Lund ruffed this with the ♠J declarer discarded the ♡4. Koltscheff then dropped the ◊Q and Lund interpreted, correctly, that West was wanting a heart switch. Lund dutifully led the ♡8 and, winning with the ♡Q, Koltscheff played his last diamond. Lund carried out the uppercut with the ♠K which cost declarer his ace and promoted two trump tricks to West. One down.

Deal Number 136

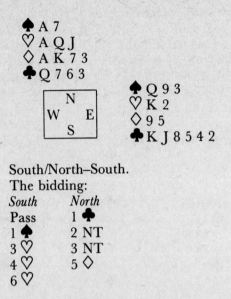

♠ A 7
♡ A Q J
◇ A K 7 3
♣ Q 7 6 3

♠ Q 9 3
♡ K 2
◇ 9 5
♣ K J 8 5 4 2

South/North–South.
The bidding:

South	North
Pass	1 ♣
1 ♠	2 NT
3 ♡	3 NT
4 ♡	5 ◇
6 ♡	

West leads the ♣10 and declarer wins with the ace. He plays a low heart to dummy's jack. How does East plan the defence?

Deal Number 137

♠ J 10 9 7
♡ A Q 6 3
◇ A Q 10
♣ Q 10

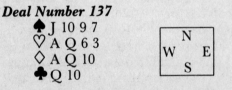

West/Both.
The bidding:

West	North	East	South
1 NT	2 NT	Double	3 ♣
Pass	Pass	Double	

What card should West lead?

Deal Number 138

♠ Q J 8
♡ A J 9 6 5
◇ K 8 2
♣ A Q

♠ 7 6 5 2
♡ K 4 3 2
◇ J 5 3
♣ K 10

South/North–South.
The bidding:

South	North
2 ♣	2 ◇
2 ♠	3 ♡
3 NT	4 ♣
4 ◇	4 NT
5 ◇	5 ♡	(East:D)
ReDouble	5 ♠
5 NT	7 ♣

West leads the ♡2. Declarer ruffs with the ♣2 and plays the ♣3. Is there any hope for the defence?

Solution Number 136

♠ A 7
♡ A Q J
◇ A K 7 3
♣ Q 7 6 3

♠ 10 8 4
♡ 10 7 5
◇ Q 10 8 4 2
♣ 10 9

McLaren
♠ Q 9 3
♡ K 2
◇ 9 5
♣ K J 8 5 4 2

♠ K J 6 5 2
♡ 9 8 6 4 3
◇ J 6
♣ A

Scottish Trials in Edinburgh, November 1975.
 Contract: 6 ♡. Lead ♣10.
 West led the ♣10. Declarer took this with the ace and then
led the ♡3 to dummy's jack. John McLaren realised that the
contract could well be ice-cold, but he was not one to give up
without a fight and calmly ducked with the ♡2. In eager
anticipation of an overtrick declarer ruffed a club so as to repeat
the trump finesse. However, McLaren won with the king and
played a third round of clubs which West ruffed with the ♡10.
Foreseeably, the contract went down one.

Solution Number 137

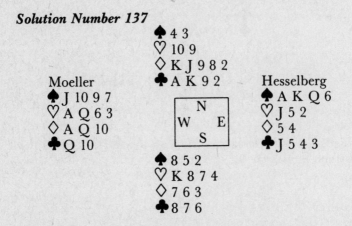

```
                    ♠ 4 3
                    ♡ 10 9
                    ◇ K J 9 8 2
                    ♣ A K 9 2
   Moeller                              Hesselberg
   ♠ J 10 9 7         ┌─────────┐       ♠ A K Q 6
   ♡ A Q 6 3          │    N    │       ♡ J 5 2
   ◇ A Q 10        W  │         │  E     ◇ 5 4
   ♣ Q 10             │    S    │       ♣ J 5 4 3
                      └─────────┘
                    ♠ 8 5 2
                    ♡ K 8 7 4
                    ◇ 7 6 3
                    ♣ 8 7 6
```

Ladies' European Championships, Elsinore, 1977.
 Contract: 3♣ doubled. Lead ♣Q.
 It is a matter perhaps for debate, but when partner doubles a
trump contract then very often a good lead is a trump card. And
Kirsten Steen Moeller led the ♣Q. Declarer won with
dummy's king and played the ♡10 to the king. West took it
with the ace and continued with the ♣10. Having won again in
dummy declarer led the ♡9 which was taken by West with the
queen. Now the ♠J was led, and then the ♠7 to East's queen.
Trine Hesselberg cashed the ♣J and played her last trump to
dummy. Dummy was endplayed by having to play a diamond.
As a result declarer could not win a trick beyond the three
trump tricks. Six down.

Garozzo
♠ Q J 8
♡ A J 9 6 5
♢ K 8 2
♣ A Q

♠ 7 6 5 2
♡ K 4 3 2
♢ J 5 3
♣ K 10

```
    N
 W     E
    S
```

♠ 4 3
♡ Q 10 8 7
♢ Q 10 6 4
♣ 7 5 4

Belladonna
♠ A K 10 9
♡ –
♢ A 9 7
♣ J 9 8 6 3 2

World Championship, Final, Bermuda, 1975.
   Contract: 7♣. Lead ♡2.
   In this final deal there arises the question of a quite imaginary defence which might possibly have completely altered the result of the World Championship. I should mention here the fact which, indeed, does not need emphasising that the 'blue' team's anchor pair, Belladonna-Garozzo, were playing with four new players in the team against North America. After 50 deals of the 96 to be played in all, the Italians were trailing with not less than 78 international match points. After 64 deals the American lead had been reduced to 46 international match points, and after 80 boards to 24 international match points. Then the Italians won the last 16 boards with 56–6 and turned a threatening defeat into a victory of 215–189 international match points.
   The grand slam in deal No. 92 gave Italy 12 international match points as North America played at 6 No Trumps at the other table. Had the slam been set, however, the result of this single board would instead, have been 17 international match points to America and the swing of 29 international match points would have turned the victory over to North America with 206–203.
   In the actual play West opened with the ♡2, which was ruffed with the ♣2 by Belladonna who then led the ♣3. As

West followed with the ♣10 Belladonna finessed luckily with the queen, and when the king fell on the ace the contract was on ice.

West can not know what the result might have been if he had without hesitation played the king on the ♣3. Had Belladonna been sitting in West's chair he would no doubt have done that. The question arises, therefore, as to whether Belladonna would have suspected West's shrewdness and would, nevertheless have drawn the queen in the third trick, or, and nobody could have blamed him, he would have instead placed East with four clubs to the 10. If the latter was the real position he could make the contract on a trump reduction play, on the condition that East was holding three spades. After reducing his trumps down to a tenace over East he would, in the eleventh trick, ruff his last spade with dummy's ♣Q. In that case, however, the grand slam would have gone down, for the obvious reason that East would have ruffed the third spade.